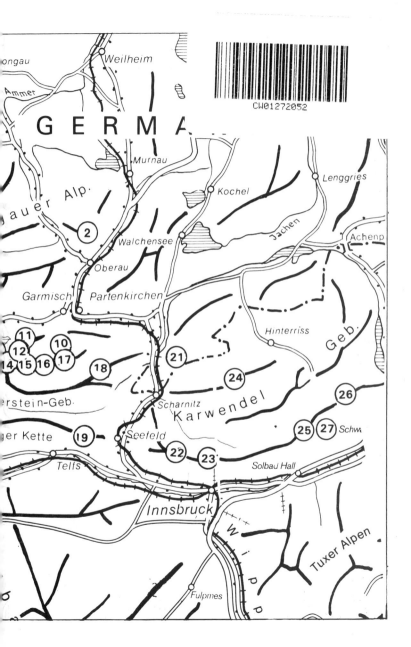

KLETTERSTEIG

Scrambles in the Northern Limestone Alps

Front Cover: On the Hindelanger Klettersteig, Allgau Alps.
Back Cover: The Nebelhorn from the Hindelanger Klettersteig.
Photos: Maurice Tedd

KLETTERSTEIG

One of the stimulating situations on the Mindelheimer Klettersteig: the smooth face of the northern Schafalpenkopf.

KLETTERSTEIG

Scrambles in the Northern Limestone Alps
Forty-four Climbing Paths

Paul Werner

Translated by
Dieter Pevsner

CICERONE PRESS,
MILNTHORPE, CUMBRIA

A selected translation from *Klettersteigfuhrer Nördliche Kalkalpen West und Osterreichische Zentralalpen* by Paul Werner, published by Bergverlag Rudolf Rother, Munich 1983.

Translated © Cicerone Press 1987

Published by Cicerone Press, 2 Police Square, Milnthorpe, Cumbria LA7 7QE

ISBN 0 902363 46 8

In this series:
Scrambles in the Lake District
Scrambles in Snowdonia
Scrambles in Skye
Scrambles in Lochaber
Via Ferrata - Scrambles in the Dolomites

CONTENTS

Introduction
- Klettersteig Protection 9
- Huts 12
- Travel 13
- Glossary 13
- Maps 14
- Climbing Paths Graded by Difficulty 14

Bavarian Pre-alps
1. Brünnstein 17
2. Ettaler Manndl 20

Allgäu alps
3. Heilbronner Weg and Hohes Licht 22
4. Mindelheim climbing path 26
5. Hindelanger climbing path 29
6. Hochvogel, Bäumenheimer Weg 35
7. Rotspitze and Breitenberg (Hohe Gänge) 37
8. Rote Flüh and Schartschrofen 39

Lechtal alps
9. Augsburger Höhenweg and Parseierspitze 43

Wetterstein
10. Alpspitze (Schöne Gänge and Mathaisenkar) 47
11. Riffelscharte 51
12. Zugspitze via Höllental 54
13. Zugspitze via Wiener Neustadt hut 58
14. Schneefernerkopf 60
15. Innere Höllentalspitze 64
16. Mit. Höllentalspitze (Jubilaumsgrat) 67
17. Hochblassen 70
18. Partenkirchener Dreitorspitze, west summit 74
19. Höhe Munde 78
20. Ehrwalder Sonnenspitze 81

Karwendel
- 21. Mittenwalder Höhenweg and Western Karwendelspitze — 87
- 22. Freiungen-Höhenweg and Reither Spitze — 90
- 23. Gipfelstürmerweg and Vordere Brandjochspitze — 94
- 24. Birkkarspitze (Brendlsteig) — 98
- 25. Grosser Bettelwurf — 102
- 26. Lamsenspitze and Hochnissl — 104
- 27. Hundskopf and Walderkammspitze — 109

Rofan
- 28. Sagzahn — 112
- 29. Guffert — 115

Kaisergebirge
- 30. Scheffauer (Widauersteig) — 121
- 31. Ellmauer Halt — 123
- 32. Hintere Goinger Halt (Steinerne Rinne) — 126
- 33. Ackerlspitze and Maukspitze — 130
- 34. Pyramidenspitze — 133

Berchtesgaden alps
- 35. Untersberg - Salzburger Hochthron (Dopplersteig and Mittagscharte) — 137
- 36. Hoher Göll (Mannlgrat) — 142
- 37. Watzmann ridge route - Mittelspitze — 145
- 38. Schönfeldspitze — 149
- 39. Hochseiler — 152
- 40. Hochkönig (southern ascents) — 156
- 41. Persailorn — 160

Dachstein
- 42. Hoher Dachstein — 165
- 43. Koppenkarstein — 169

Salzkammergut
- 44. Traunstein — 172

Introduction

EVEN before the turn of the century, when the opening up of the Eastern Alps to tourists was completed and the number of mountaineers increased by leaps and bounds, a start was made on reducing the difficulty of specific hard sections of popular climbs by means of wire ropes and iron rungs. The first protection in the gap between the summits of the Grossglockner (1869!), the Heilbron Way in the Allgau (1899) and the Eggersteig in the Wilder Kaiser (1903) originated thus. The advance into acknowledged climbing-grounds followed, with the building of the Pössnecker Path on the west flank of the Sella. After the First World War, military routes with fixtures, such as the Alpini Way in the Sexten Dolomites, were also put at the service of the mountaineer.

However, the real development of protected climbing routes did not begin until the thirties, when the S.A.T. (Societá Alpinistica Trentina), an independent mountaineering club from Trent, together with the C.A.I. (Club Alpino Italiano), shortened and made easier the time-consuming approaches to popular climbing routes in the Brenta, by installing artificial aids. This was the beginning of the Bochette Way, which was continued after the Second World War in work covering many years, and which soon achieved great celebrity. The boldness of the route and its alpine beauty were discovered by numerous mountain walkers, although, following its builders' intention, it does not touch any summits. The Bochette Way became the model for further installations of the same kind, although the original principle - not to build such artificial routes to summits - was soon broken. Recently opinions have been expressed in the C.A.I. that all new installation of 'iron ways' should be forbidden, which understandably has led to vigorous and continuing debate.

The climbing aids (wire ropes, rungs, pegs, ladders) which have been fixed with great effort and skill on difficult, sometimes vertical, and even overhanging rock, enable even non-climbers to do routes which formerly were Grades III, IV and V. So theoretically any plain-dweller in reasonable physical training and active in sports could successfully tackle a climbing path without further ado. But two conditions must be fulfilled without qualification: absolute freedom from dizziness, and a certain degree of mountain experience, including not only sure-footedness but also an awareness of alpine dangers. Mountain experience is acquired almost automatically through a series of trips, but feelings of dizziness are constitutional and cannot always be overcome by slow habituation of looking steeply down. So anyone who is not completely certain on this point should go only with a guide or a reliable companion.

Effective protection on climbing paths is as follows: a belay rope about 3 metres long is attached to the harness (or tied round the waist) in such a way that there are two ropes each of an arm's length. To the end of each rope a sling is attached on each of which is clipped a karabiner. These used in turn enable one to clip on to the wire rope, and thus, at least on a traverse or a rope that does not run too steeply, one has optimal self-protection. Two karabiners are used because with only one the climber would NOT be protected when passing anchorages on the fixed rope. With two, one is already placed beyond the anchor-peg when you have to unclip in order to pass it, and thus serves as self-protection.

If the fixed rope runs vertically, the self-belay method described cannot be used, because in the case of a fall the karabiners would be strained to bending-point and could break. Instead climb with a 11mm rope (30m. is long enough) as on a climbing-route, bearing in mind the usual belaying methods (self-belay and second's belay). The anchorage points of the fixed rope now offer superb running belays and stance belays, which are comparable with peg belays in climbing.

Mastery of today's methods of protection should of course be taken for granted for the 'climbing-path' walker. Study the relevant textbooks and if possible gain practical experience on a climbing-wall (or during a basic course on rock). The use of a helmet is as important as effective belaying.

The protected paths should be used only in good weather conditions. As their Italian name, - Via Ferrata, iron way - betrays, they are pretty ferruginous and therefore genuine lightning conductors in thunderstorms. If one is nevertheless surprised by a mountain thunderstorm (and these develop uncommonly quickly, especially in high summer) - then keep away from the iron ladders and wire ropes! Even though the artificial protection on such routes in the Dolomites is usually in good condition (in many other East Alpine mountain groups protection, fixed umpteen years ago, is often neglected, because no one bothers about it any longer), nevertheless one must test each rung etc. for firmness before putting weight on it, just as the climber tests his hold, for naturally its security in the rock can be damaged by the weather. Further - a fixed rope should always be used by one person at a time, because the unequal pull on the rope can jerk one off one's balance.

Experienced mountain walkers can be assumed to know about normal equipment, the alpine distress signal and the like. In the text attention is drawn to peculiarities of individual routes. A bivouac sack or at least a large poly bag should be taken on longer routes and those leading to greater heights.

Klettersteig Protection
The growing popularity of climbing paths (Klettersteig or Via Ferrata) has led to a technical discussion on the best method of protection. Two well-known guide-book writers contributed the following to *Climber & Rambler* (now *Climber*) magazine:

> One spectacular difference between walking or scrambling in the Alps and in Britain is the audacity of Via Ferrata. Furnished with metal ladders and wire ropes - easing technical difficulty if not the the breathtaking exposure - these routes attack some astonishingly steep faces, sometimes for many hundreds of feet. *Gladys Sellers* outlines the necessary equipment for self protection on these iron stairways:
>
> The essential difference between a Via Ferrata and a rock climb is that the Ferrata is provided with protection and assistance such as wire cables, steel ladders or hoops according to the situation. The climber wears a harness of some sort and attaches him/herself to this protection by means of a karabiner on the end of a short length of rope.
>
> It is common practice to wear a chest harness - these keep you upright in the event of a minor fall - and helmets are not generally worn. Climbers will be uneasy to say the least about using a chest harness and with good cause. After a fall that leaves the climber hanging free, paralysis of the arms takes place within 10-20 minutes and that means the victim will no longer be able to help him/herself. Internal injuries follow and death within 2½ hours. Pretty thoughts, but a much longer survival time than that given by a rope around the waist. I've tried to remember all the tricky situations I've been in, usually on iron hoops, when a fall could result in hanging free out of reach of quick help. I can't think of any in five Via Ferrata holidays, so I conclude the risks are acceptably small.

The most popular chest harness in the Dolomites is Edelrid's, simply because Germans outnumber any other nationality. It is not stocked in this country, but Edelrid's agent assures me that any good climbing shop can get it provided the required size is known. To inspect and try on a chest harness the climber will have to go to a shop selling caving tackle, for cavers use chest harnesses. These are usually found in the Craven district of the Yorkshire Dales, the Peak District and South Wales. These shops usually stock at least Troll's Standard Chest Harness, available in sizes 32" to 44" and Petzl's Classique Chest Harness. These two harnesses use stiff tape instead of stitched rope around the chest, and Troll's can be fitted with leg loops.

Whatever harness is used the two ends of it are tied together with about 2 metres of 7 or 9mm rope using a bowline and stopper knot. If two ropes are used they are tied in one knot. It is good practice to use two ropes if the route is a difficult one or the climber inexperienced. This is not a belt and brace attitude, but as the karabiner must be removed from and re-attached to the protection at frequent intervals, sometimes in difficult and exposed situations, the climber is never left without protection. See diagrams. The karabiner should be a wide gated one but not screw gated. The standard karabiner will fit cables and some ladders but does not open wide enough to go onto iron hoops. Sod's Law says that iron hoops are used in just those places where you want protection most. Not all wide gate karabiners are wide enough but the Bonaiti 2700Kg model is suited to all needs. Not available in every shop.

Chris Wright adds the following:

I would endorse the use of a chest harness in preference to a waist belt or sit harness if only because the point of attachment is closer to the fixed ropes: a waist attachment requires about 1.5m of sling. I use Troll's Freestyle Chest Harness without the plastic gear loops.

The more usual Continental practice when using a rope as a sling attachment is to tie into the chest harness by a figure of 8 from the centre of the rope, rather than by bowline as described and illustrated in the article. The ends are tied on to the krabs by figures of 8 as illustrated. The disadvantage of the 8-tie on is that all the knots have to be undone when putting on or taking off the harness.

INTRODUCTION

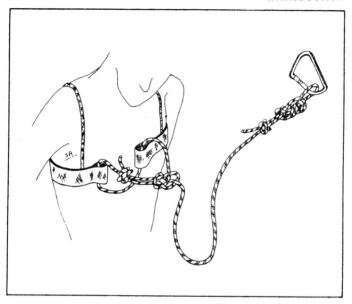

Chest harness connection for klettersteig protection.

An alternative to 7 or 9mm rope is to use two stitched tape slings - Troll Snake Slings, medium length (910mm) in 15mm supertape have a breaking strength of 1000kg each. The krabs slip easily into the stitched loops, and better than knots, do not snag in the fixed rope pitons or get trapped between rock face and fixed rope when the cable is under tension. I know that it is not recommended practice to use even a screwgate krab in a chest harness, but three-point loading is not so critical on Via Ferratas where, if you do slip and fall, you are only likely to fall a few feet, unlike in free climbing where the run-out between points of protection may be considerable. As an alternative to a screwgate krab on the chest harness you can use a Petzl Delta Maillon Rapide, which can be loaded in any direction. The alloy type has a breaking strength of 2000kg, steel 4500kg. (Available from any caving suppliers, or Lyon Equipment, Dent.)

Both Clog and Stubai make widegate snap krabs, which are more widely available than the Bonaiti. Mine are Stubai 'Klettersteig' of 2200kg strength.

KLETTERSTEIG

Using the protection on a ladder, left, and cable, right.

I would dispute the statement that helmets are not generally worn. In recent years helmet use has been more widespread. In early season ice and stonefalls are frequent, and anyone caught behind an excited, jabbering party of Italian tourists at any time will be aware of the regularity of stones being dislodged from ledges and gullies.

Finally, an item of protective gear that has been overlooked. An old pair of leather gardening or ski gloves will protect the hands from those broken strands of wire cable, and make it more comfortable when the Via Ferrata is iced up.

(Reproduced by permission of the authors and Climber magazine.)

Huts

The mountain huts are open to all; most of them provide both food and shelter. Members of the various alpine clubs pay reduced rates for accommodation, but not food. Three types of accommodation are available, abbreviated thus in the text: **B** - Beds (separate bunk beds in special rooms); **M** - Matratzenlager (the usual dormitory style

INTRODUCTION

accommodation. Mixed sexes). L - Lager (this should strictly be Notlager; emergency bedding on the floor or in the winter room).

Some small huts and winter rooms are unwardened and admittance is by key obtainable to members only. Further details from the Austrian Alpine Club, 13 Longcroft House, Fretherne Road, Welwyn Garden City, Herts AL8 6PQ (Tel: 07073-24835)

Travel

Air: Many flights each day from several British airports to Munich, the overall centre for the region. Flights also from Gatwick to Innsbruck (Thurs, Fri, Sat) and Heathrow to Salzburg (Fri, Sat, Sun). Linz can also be reached by changing at Frankfurt.

Rail: Excellent rail services from Munich throughout the area, supplemented by post buses. The following centres might be found convenient: Oberstdorf (Allgauer); Garmisch-Partenkirchen (Wetterstein); Innsbruck (Karwendel); Kufstein (Kaisergebirge); Berchtesgaden (Berchtesgaden Alps).

Road: The autobahn system either reaches or comes within a few miles of all the places named above. A useful road map is Kummerly & Frey Austria 1/500,000.

Glossary

GERMAN	ENGLISH
Alpe, Almhütte	alp, alm-hut
Band	ledge
Berg	mountain
Bergrettung	Mountain Rescue
Bezeichnung	way-marking
Biwakschachtel	bivouac-box
Ebene, Hochfläche	level tract, plateau
Eis	ice
Fels, Stein	rock, stone
Felswand	cliff, wall
Gefahr	danger
Gefährlich	dangerous
Gipfel, Spitze	summit
Gletscher	glacier
Grat	ridge, arête
Griff	hold
Hilfe!	Help!
Hügel	hill (N.B.!)
Hütte, Haus	mountain hut
Kar, kessel	corrie, basin, combe
Klammern	iron rungs
Latschen	pine scrub
Leiter	ladder
links	(to the) left
Nadel	needle, pinnacle
Pass, Joch	pass
rechts	(to the) right
Rücken	ridge
Sattel	saddle, pass
Scharte	small pass, gap
Schlucht	gorge, ravine
Schutt, Geröl	scree
Schwierig	difficult
See	lake
Seil, Kabel	rope
Spitze, Gipfel	summit
Steinschlag	stone-fall
Tal	valley
Tritt	foothold
Unterstand	dug-out (military)
Verschneidung	Dièrdre
Vorbau, Sockel	base, plinth
Wand	wall, cliff
Wegteilung	path, junction

Maps

Kompass Wanderkarte 1/50,000 cover the area in a number of sheets. W to E the relevant sheets are:
Routes 3,4,5,6,7, K3 Allgauer Alpen-Kl.Walsertal
Route 9 K34 Landeck-N.Samnaungruppe
Route 8 K4 Fusen-Ausserfern
Routes 10,11,12,13,14,15,16,17,18,19,20 K25 Ehrwald-Lermoos-Miemingerkette
Route 2 K7 Murnau-Kochel-Staffelsee
Routes 21,22,23,24,25,26,27 K26 Karwendelgebirge
Route 28 K27 Achensee-Rofangebirge
Route 29 K8 Tegernsee-Schliersee
Routes 1,30,31,32,33,34 K9 Kaisergebirge
Routes 35,36,37 K14 Berchtesgadener Land-Chiemgau
Routes 38,41 K30 Saalfelden-Leoganger Steinberge
Routes 39,40 K15 Tennengebirge-Hochkonig
Routes 42,43 K31 Radstadt-Schladming
Route 44 K19 Almtal-Kremstal

Maps available from: McCarta Ltd., 122 King's Cross Road, London, WC1X 9DS. (Telephone: 01-278-8278)
Edward Stanford Ltd., 27a Floral Street, London, WC2E 9LP. (Telephone 01-836-1321)

Climbing paths graded by difficulty

The grades used here bear no relation to the familiar climbers' scale (Grades I-VI). But it may be useful to compare them with the grades used by Hilde Frass in *Via Ferrata: Scrambles in the Dolomites*, translated by Cecil Davies (Cicerone Press 1982). The later routes under B and all those under C roughly correspond to the Italian ones which Frau Frass grades a). My grade D roughly corresponds to her grades b) and c).

A   Easy mountain tours up to 2000m with short wire rope sections, requiring some freedom from vertigo. Ideal trial runs for climbing path novices:
   1. Brünnstein
   2. Ettaler Manndl
   7. Rotspitze and Breitenberg

27. Hundskopf
28. Sagzahn
34. Pyramidenspitze
35. Untersberg-Salzburger Hochthron
44. Traunstein

B   Tours above 2000m with short climbing path sections, requiring freedom from vertigo and surefootedness, but in some cases, because the ascents are long, also requiring a fair degree of stamina:
    8. Rote Flüh, Schartschrofen
   11. Riffelscharte
   14. Schneefernerkopf
   19. Hohe Munde-Niedere Munde
   22. Freiungen-Höhenweg, Reither Spitze
   23. Gipfelstürmerweg, Vordere Brandjochspitze
   24. Birkkarspitze (Brendlsteig)
   29. Guffert, Nordansteig

C   Tours with longer climbing path sections requiring not only greater freedom from vertigo, but also stamina, mountain experience and route-finding skill:
    3. Heilbronner Weg.
    6. Hochvogel (Baümenheimer Weg)
   15. Innere Höllentalspitze
   18. Partenkirchener Dreitorspitze, West summit
   21. Mittenwalder Höhenweg
   25. Bettelwurf
   26. Lamsenspitze and Hochnissl
   30 Scheffauer (Widauersteig)
   32. Hintere Goinger Halt, (Steinerne Rinne)
   33. Ackerlspitze
   36. Hoher Göll (Mannlgrat)
   38. Schönfeldspitze
   41. Persailhorn
   43. Koppenkarstein

D   High alpine tours with long and advanced climbing path sections, of which parts may require absolute freedom from vertigo. Some of these tours also require exceptional stamina if undertaken without overnight stops:
    4. Mindelheimer Klettersteig

5. Hindelanger Klettersteig
9. Augsburger Höhenweg
10. Alpspitze
12. Zugspitze via Höllental
13. Zugspitze via Wiener Neustadt hut
16. Jubiläumsweg
31. Ellmauer Halt (Gamsängersteig)
37. Watzmann Ridge route
39. Hochseiler (Mooshammersteig)
40. Hochkönig (south ascents)
42. Hoher Dachstein

E Tours which cross the divide between climbing paths and rock-climbing (up to Grade II), requiring not only absolute surefootedness and freedom from vertigo, but also some measure of climbing skills:
17. Hochblassen
20. Ehrwalder Sonnenspitze
39. Hochseiler (Mooshammersteig and descent to Torscharte)

Bavarian Pre-Alps

1. BRÜNNSTEIN 1620m
Bayrischzell Hills

The Julius Mayr climbing path from the Brünnsteinhaus to the summit was equipped as long ago as 1898. It offers some delightful wire rope sections and, as the easiest of all the climbing paths in this book, makes an ideal trial-run for beginners. Both the routes up to the Brünnsteinhaus are pleasant, with plenty of variety, and the view to the Wilder Kaiser is sure to whet your appetite for other, more daring, ventures.

Approaches
a) By car the best approach is from the old mountain inn, the Feuriger Tatzelwurm (Fiery Dragon) (765m), on the panoramic road from Bayrischzell across the Sudelfeld.
b) By train, approach from Oberau (480m) on the Rosenheim-Kufstein line.

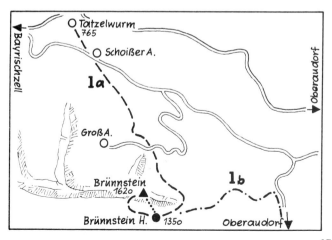

The shoulder-width rock cleft at the start of the Julius-Mayr-Weg.

Ascents to the Brünnsteinhaus
a) The quickest way up begins at the large carpark a few hundred metres above the Tatzelwurm, where there is also a panoramic diagram in a little shelter. Cross the Schoisseralm (950m), then walk north-east on gently-rising forest paths half-way round the Brünnstein to the Brünsteinhaus.
b) Walk through Oberaudorf to the delightful little Luegsteinsee and straight on to the Gasthaus Gfallermühle. Now walk west along a little road through Mühlau and almost to Rechenau. Fork right to the Wildgrubhöfe, then follow the waymarked path to the Brünnsteinhaus.

Summit ascent
From the hut follow the steep forest path up for a few minutes to a 25-metre cleft in the rock. Squeeze through, and 30 mins easy, amusing scrambling up the wire ropes will take you to the summit chapel.

Descents
As ascents: but from the summit down to Brünnsteinhaus there is an easier path down the west side.

Difficulty
Easy mountain tour. A measure of freedom from vertigo required for the summit ascent.

Times
Tatzelwurm - Brünnsteinhaus 2 hrs: Oberaudorf - Brünnsteinhaus 3 hrs: summit ascent ¾ hr: descents 1 hr less in each case: Tatzelwurm -Oberaudorf 2 hrs.

Base
Brünnsteinhaus (1350m): service year round: 18B, 70M.

Altitude differences
Tatzelwurm - Brünnsteinhaus 585m; Oberaudorf - Brünnsteinhaus 870m: Brünnsteinhaus - summit 270m.

Climbing path altitude
c.230m.

Note
It is well worth making the small detour to see the pretty gorge and waterfall above the Tatzelwurm

2. ETTALER MANNDL 1633m
Eastern Ammergau Alps

This handsome, jagged rock outcrop rises above wooded hills and dominates the view by the Garmisch road just south of Murnau. With its little wire rope section, it makes a gentle one-day outing and an ideal climbing-path trial for novices and children.

Approach
Via Ettal or Oberammergau. The best way from Munich and the north is by the Garmisch autobahn and, from where it ends, the B2 (Olympiastrasse) to the turn-off at Oberau. If you like the easy life or late starts, you can whisk up to the Laber by the Oberammergau gondola cableway (from 9 a.m.).

Ascent to the Laber and the summit rocks
a) The shortest route is from the monastery at Ettal. It starts at the north-east corner of the monastery wall, then goes through meadows into the forest and up the steep, densely wooded southern side of the ravine.

   The clearly-waymarked path gets steeper and, after passing a hunting box, reaches the Tiefentaler Sattel (saddle), and a first view of the Staffelsee.

   3½ km from Ettal the path joins the main track from the Laber to the Manndl rocks. At the foot of the vertical south wall of the Manndl, turn right to the normal entry at the south-east foot of the summit rocks.
b) From Oberammergau, follow the comfortable track from the lower station of the cableway for about 700m to a forest road, then go straight along a steep path through the Laber woods, over the Laber alm and the Schartenkopf col to the upper cableway station on the Laber (1675m: lovely views from the upper section of the path).
c) As b) as far as the forest road. Then follow this waymarked, almost level, and rather boring road as far as the Bärenbadfleck. Now turn right up a meadow and follow a way-marked path to the junction with the Laber - Ettaler Manndl path beside an idyllic little lake called the Soilasee. From here the Manndl is 1km, the Laber 1½km. Both paths are highly recommended.
d) If you have come up the cableway, then you have no more than a comfortable stroll along the lovely path from the Laber, first more or less downhill as far as the junction with the Ettal path,

then gently uphill for the last 200m to the summit rocks.

Summit ascent
Up the south wall on continuous wire ropes in about 15 easy and enjoyable minutes. Expect crowds at autumn weekends!

Descents
As ascents.

Difficulty
Easy day outing. Freedom from vertigo required for summit ascent. Beginners and children should be roped.

Times
From Ettal or Oberammergau 2½hrs: descents 1 hr less: upper cableway station to Manndl rocks c.½ hr: summit ascent ¼ hr.

Base
Upper station of Oberammergau - Laber cableway (1675m): service all year; no overnight facilities.

Altitude differences
Ettal - summit 745m: Oberammergau - summit 795m.

Climbing path altitude
c.60m.

Note
Be sure to visit the famous monastery church at Ettal - a perfect jewel of Bavarian baroque architecture. The Passion Play theatre at Oberammergau is open daily throughout the year (conducted tours) 9-12 and 13.30-16.30. The tour takes 20 mins. and the maximum wait is 15 mins.

Allgäu Alps

3. HEILBRONNER WEG AND HOHES LICHT 2651m
Allgäu Alps, main ridge

I can think of no better start than to quote a well-known German mountaineering writer, Alois Haydn:

> The Heilbronner Weg is over 70 years old. It cannot compete in length or daring with newer climbing paths, yet this old favourite is as well loved today as ever it was. And rightly so, for it still offers better sport and wider variety than all the many other high-altitude routes in the Allgäu Alps

I would recommend that you walk from E to W (as in the following description) rather than *vice versa*, for two good reasons. First, because that way your ascent of the Hohes Licht (the second highest peak of the Allgäu Alps) will come on the morning of the second day, when you will have the benefit of shade: secondly, because the Rappensee hut is a lot less cramped than the others on the route.

Approaches
a) I recommend Oberstdorf im Allgäu (815m). It is the favourite valley start for all excursions that include the Heilbronner Weg because there are convenient routes back to Oberstdorf from both ends of the climbing path.
b) A second possibility is Lechleiten (1541m) at the head of the Lech valley (in the Austrian Tyrol).

Ascent to the Rappensee hut
a) From Oberstdorf walk or take a horse-drawn carriage to Einodsbach (1113m, the southernmost community in Germany). Car drivers staying at least three nights in local hotels (but not huts!) can apply to the Oberstdorf council office (Sachsenweg 2) for a permit to drive on this road. Alternatively there is a bus as far as Birgsau. The easy, clearly-waymarked path begins at the inn at Einodsbach, crosses the bridge over the stream from the Bacherloch (1093m), then climbs through woods and leads across the Bachreineralp (1129m) and the Petersalp (1296m), to reach the Enzian hut (1710m: sevice but no overnight facilities) in 2½

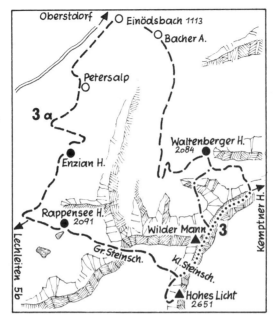

hrs. Now up in hairpins, across some steep ribs, up to the saddle and round the back of the Seebichl to the hut. (Overnight stop recommended.)

b) From Lechleiten the easy, waymarked path starts at the Holzgauerhaus and heads north-west to the Lechleiten alp (1783m: ½ hr), then goes up the eastern slopes of a wide saddle called Am Schänzle, climbs to the highest point on the Schlosswand (1876m) and levels off to cross the Obere Biberalp. From here the route goes down into the deep ravine of the Mutzentobel, round the western slopes of the Rappenköpfl to the Schafalp, then gently up into the wide combe crossed by the stream running down from the Rappensee. Now cross the Kobertobel, climb up the southern slope of the Mutzenkopf and over to the saddle (1919m) where you will join path a) from Oberstdorf. Note that the Mutzentobel is only partly protected by wire ropes. In wet or snowy conditions it becomes perilously slippery and must then be attempted only by experienced scramblers.

Summit ascent and ridge route

From the Rappensee hut first make for the Grosse Steinscharte (2262m), then cross a combe, over scree and boulders, and a gully (wire ropes) to the beginning of the route to the summit of the Hohes Licht. If the weather is clear, do not miss the 30 mins ascent to the summit for the magnificent views (1¾ hrs from the hut). Now return to the junction, which is the beginning of the Heilbronner Weg proper. Start through the narrow cleft called the Heilbronner Törl, then go carefully (especially in early summer) over the rock slabs up to the Kleine Steinscharte (2541m; ½ hr).

Now cross the ridge to the sunny south-side and a fine view of the Lechtal Alps. Climb the crags of the Steinschartenkopf on the 15m steel ladder and a few minutes' easy walk will take you to the summit (2615m). Continue along the ridge, then over scree and rock round the right-hand side of the Wilder Mann (2577m). Summit-baggers can pick up this one at the cost of a few extra minutes.

From the next gap (Socktalscharte, 2446m) there is a steep emergency route down to the Waltenberger Haus (hut) (1 hr). But if the weather is adequate, then continue to the Bockkarkopf (2608m) and enjoy a sequence of vertiginous views down onto the latter hut.

The ridge continues its varied way, via the Western Bockkarscharte, then another (unnamed) gap and, after a stretch where the path runs beneath huge rock overhangs, the Eastern Bockkarscharte. At this point a bronze plaque marks the end of the Heilbronner Weg proper, but a lovely high-level path continues to the Kempten hut. This is not in any sense a climbing path, but it is by far the most interesting of all the possible descents.

Descents

a) If you decide for the path to the Kempten hut, you will soon find yourself in a totally different landscape. The path crosses the gently-rounded southern slopes of the Hochfrottspitze and the harmless snowfield of the Schwarze Milz, where a sign marks the start of the waymarked route to the summit of the Mädelegabel (2645m: reckon 1 hr). But our route goes straight on, through rock-fall boulders, then levels off beside a little lake (the Schwarzmilzsee) and crosses the flat Mergelböden to the Oberes Mädelejoch (1968m). Now swing gradually to the north and you will soon see the Kempten hut in the distance. It is possible to get down to Spielmannsau and back to Oberstdorf within the day, but it would require considerable stamina, so I strongly recommend a second overnight stop.

ALLGÄU ALPS ROUTE 3

b) From the Eastern Bockkarscharte take the clearly-waymarked path heading north. It winds in steep hairpins, first over rock, then over scree and some snow-fields, down to the Waltenberger Haus which stands on a magnificent site at the edge of the Bockkar, surrounded by towering mountains and almost leaning over the precipice that falls to the Bacherloch below. If the weather permits, it is worth taking the short path north from the hut to look at the formidable west face of the Trettachspitze. The descent from the Waltenberger Haus is by the steep path which goes first down the impressive gorge (wire ropes where the rock is wet), then crosses through the wild scenery of the Bacherloch and finally goes over the Bacheralp (1174m) and back to Einodsbach (1½ hrs).

Difficulty

High alpine ridge route. With overnight stop at Rappensee hut, moderately strenuous. Without stop, very arduous. If weather shows signs of deteriorating, descend at earliest opportunity! Requires surefootedness and freedom from vertigo. In snow, should be attempted only by experienced scramblers. In normal conditions, however, no technical problems.

Times

Einodsbach - Rappensee hut 3½ hrs: Lechleiten - Rappensee hut 2½ hrs: Rappensee hut - Grosse - and Kleine Steinscharte - Eastern Bockkarscharte 3-3½ hrs: Eastern Bockkarscharte - Kempten hut 2¼ hrs: descent from ridge to Waltenberger Haus 1 hr; Waltenberger Haus - Einodsbach 1½ hrs.

Bases

Rappensee hut (2091m); service 20/6 - 15/10; 42B, 190M, 100L. Waltenberger Haus (2084m); service Whitsun - 1/10; 10B, 60M. Kempten Hut (1846m); service 15/6 - mid-Oct: 85B, 220M. Enzian hut (1710m); service; no overnight facilities.

Altitude Differences

Oberstdorf - Einodsbach 300m; Einodsbach - Rappenseehut 978m; Rappenseehut - Hohes Licht 560m.

Length of climbing path

c.5 km.

KLETTERSTEIG

4. MINDELHEIM CLIMBING PATH, INCLUDING NORTHERN SCHAFALPENKOPF 2320m
Allgäu Alps

This route over the Schafalpenköpfe - a section of the high-level route called the Grosser Allgäuer Höhenweg - took three years to create and was opened in 1975. By comparison with most of the climbing paths in the northern limestone Alps, this is a real surprise, a demanding 'iron way' offering two full hours on the wild, shattered rocks of a complicated ridge and looking across to the great buttresses of the main ridge of the Allgäu Alps. In those two hours it shows off the whole gamut of the climbing-path-builder's art, and its delights compare favourably with the best that the *vie ferrate* of the Dolomites can offer.

Approaches
a) From Oberstdorf, as for Route No.3.
b) Both the possible base huts are within fairly easy distance of Mittelberg in the Kleines Walsertal (1219m).

Ascent to the Mindelheim hut
a) From Mittelberg, up the Wildental and over the Hintere Wildenalm (3 hrs).
b) From Mittelberg, up the Gemstelbachtal and over the Hintere Gemstelalm (4½ hrs).
c) From Birgsau (949m), up the Rappenalptal (4 hrs). Take the bus or horse-drawn carriage as far as Birgsau, then walk 7 km of metalled road to the foot of the path to the hut.
d) From the Rappensee hut, via Mutzentobel, Biberalpe and Schrofenpass (3-4 hrs).

Ascent to the Fiderepass hut
a) From Mittelberg, up the Wildental (3 hrs).
b) From the upper station of either the Fellhorn cable-way or the Kanzelwand cableway and over the Kügundalpe (2 hrs either route).
c) From the lower station of the Fellhorn cableway take the footpath (red and green waymarks) heading towards the Kanzelwandhaus (hut). Follow it to the metalled road that leads up to the alp, then take the road as far as the Schlappoldhöfle and from there a path via the Warmatsgundalpe and the Kühgund to the Fiderepass (3¾ hrs).

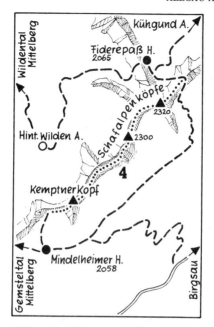

d) Take the Söllereck cableway, and from the Hotel Schönblick at the top take the path to the Fiderepass via Söllereck, Schlappold, Fellhorn and Kühgundalpe (4½ hrs).
e) A very enjoyable approach for experienced and confident walkers goes via the Kanzelwand cableway, and then to the Fiderepass over the tops of the Schüsser, Hochgehrenspitze and Hammerspitze (3 hrs).

Ridge route
From the Fiderepass walk to the Saubuckelscharte (½ hr). From here the path drops a little to a signboard, then climbs right and up to the northern cliffs of the Northern Schafalpenkopf (2320m). There are two long ladders and some wire ropes to help you up the steep ascent into the gap near the summit. Cross to the south side, traverse a rock face (wire ropes) and climb another ladder onto the level ridge, where you cross a small but very deep rock crevasse on a somewhat windy steel bridge. Now follow the wire ropes steeply down into a gap, and cross to the south-east side. Just before you get into the combe, climb

west up more wire ropes, then 20m down a very exposed vertical wall on iron rungs. The next section - the steep ascent to the Middle Schafalpenkopf (2300m) - is the finest, but also the most awkward and exposed of the whole tour. Climb a small chimney to pass a rock step, then turn west and traverse up steep rock walls on iron pegs and wire ropes. The summit is reached by way of a steel bridge and some steep rock steps. From the top follow the hairpins down 150m through the grass to the next depression. The next ascent, to the Southern Schafalpenkopf, is well protected. The lower part of the climb goes mostly up the west side of the ridge. Higher up the route keeps more to the south-east side to take you fairly harmlessly to the summit (2275m). Now make your way down to the grassy ridge, either down the hairpin path, or, a little to the south-west, down a very steep but protected rock gully. That leaves only a brief coda: the path takes in the summit cross of the Kemptner Kopflë, giving a view down to the Mindelheim hut which is your goal.

Descent
As Ascents. You can return to your starting hut in ease and comfort to the east of the ridge by the waymarked path which connects the two huts roughly along the 1900m line.

Difficulty
A technically demanding ridge route with some very exposed sections. Protection is adequate and perfectly designed, but not excessive. You will require freedom from vertigo and surefootedness in very high degree. If you are less than perfectly confident, use self-belays. Possible in mist, but inadvisable in rain, when areas of wet clay along the route become perilously slippery.

Times
Climbing path from either hut to the other 3-3½ hrs. For other times see descriptions of ascents to huts.

Bases
Mindelheim hut (2058m); service mid-June - end-Sept; 200 bed-spaces of all kinds: winter shelter in old building accessible with Alpine Club key, 12L. Fiderepass hut (2065m); service Whitsun - mid-Oct; 20B, 100M; no winter shelter.

Altitude differences
Mittelberg - Mindelheim hut or Fiderepass hut c.840m; Birgsau - Mindelheim hut or Fiderepass hut c.1210m; either hut - Northern Schafalpenkopf c.260m.

Climbing path length
c.5 km, but many ups and downs.

5: HINDELANGER KLETTERSTEIG
(Western Wengenkopf) 2235m
Allgäu Alps

The Hindelang climbing path was constructed between 1973 and 1978 by the Hindelang group of the Allgäu-Immenstadt section of the DAV (German Alpine Club). It runs from the Nebelhorn to the Grosser Daumen across the wild clefts of a rocky ridge with a number of towering pinnacles, of which the two Wengenköpfe are the most prominent.

Modern technology has given easy access to the starting point on the Nebelhorn, so, by contrast with the old Heilbronner Weg (Route 3) and the Mindelheimer Klettersteig (Route 4), there are no long approach walks to huts or problems with overnight accommodation, and the only ascents are counter-climbs. But although this makes the Hindelanger Klettersteig much frequented, it should not be regarded as a suitable excursion for beginners or inexperienced scramblers. Protection has been kept to the essential minimum, and there are sheer drops on either side of some unprotected and very narrow sections of the ridge, so you will need absolute freedom from vertigo. Experienced climbing path enthusiasts will find this route a comparatively easy treat: a sometimes acrobatic but technically simple and enjoyable scramble from the ridge up to peaks and from the peaks back to the gaps below, with the added bonus of magnificent panoramas across the high alps between the Hohes Licht and the Zugspitze and sweeping views across the pre-alpine plain. But it is also worth consideration by any mountain walkers who feel ready for an extra thrill, because there are several easy escape routes off the ridge, and the return journey presents no problems at all.

Approach
From Oberstdorf (see Route 3), via the lower station of the Nebelhorn cableway.

Ascent of the Nebelhorn
a) Take the Nebelhorn cableway past the intermediate station at the Seealpe to the top at the Berghotel Nebelhorn (1929m) and the neighbouring Edmund-Probst-Haus hut (1925m). Now take the chair-lift past an intermediate station (Koblatt) onto the Nebelhorn (summit hut with restaurant, 2224m). The cableway runs from 0800 to 1700.
b) Walk up the track to the Vordere Seealpe (1280m). Follow a wide

KLETTERSTEIG

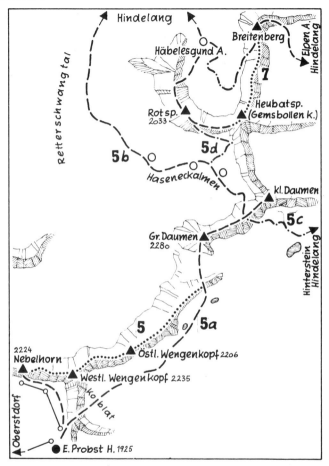

path along the Faltenbach stream to the upper station of the cableway, then a track up to the Koblatt, and finally a path up to the summit. (4-5hrs!)

Ridge route
A few minutes walk from the cableways station, over the first hump of the ridge, will take you to the bronze plaque which marks the entrance

to the climbing path. Climb the first, rather exposed, ladder up a prominent pinnacle and follow the unprotected rock ridge northwards to the first depression. The next stretch is comfortable walking. Beyond it, follow the cable down a simple rock step onto a flat, grassy hump. The short, somewhat alarming stretch of rock which follows, over a narrow and only intermittently protected section of ridge, requires some degree of climbing skill (Grade I, in parts Grade II). While you are negotiating it, you will probably scarcely notice that you have climbed up and over the highest point on the tour - the Western Wengenkopf (2235m). After a harmless stretch of ridge, the route takes a well protected dip over rock into a gap, then crosses a very exposed and at first unprotected length of ridge. Now climb down two vertical ladders onto the west side of the ridge and make an exposed traverse along a smooth, vertical wall across to the next grassy stretch of ridge. Where it dips in the middle, a sign marks the start of the first escape route, eastwards down to the Koblatt. Our route soon reaches its longest ladder - which slants up over a deep cleft. Now cross a harmless grassy area, then negotiate another narrow but protected piece of ridge and climb gently up over some rock slabs. The following section goes up and down like a switchback, and alternates between narrow, protected lengths of sharp ridge and stretches of wider, often positively comfortable path. Some exciting acrobatics will take you across a length of wild and shattered ridge to an unexpected ladder down a steep and, in parts, extremely exposed pitch. From the bottom, a very narrow path down the steep side of the ridge leads to a deep, grassy gap. Beyond the gap, the route begins another interesting but well protected climb, beyond which you reach a second grassy gap - just about half-way along the climbing path - where a sign marks the start of the easy second escape route down to the Koblatt. Now climb again, up another ladder, then on steel cables over a small rock pinnacle. The next gap will reward you with an enchanting view down to the first of a series of vivid emerald green tarns. After a climb down another vertical ladder you will see two more of them, in the desolate combe far below. Next cross a last section of ridge and climb a final ladder onto the Eastern Wengenkopf (2206m), and scramble down to the lowest point of the whole tour, where another bronze plaque marks the beginning of a third unmarked but easy route leading down to the Koblatt. Now an astonishing piece of protection will loft you with surprising ease over the top of the next rock pinnacle. Scramble down the other side along a narrow unprotected ledge, and you will soon reach the spot, directly above the Laufbichelsee, where the climbing path ends and you join the walkers' path at a signpost

*On the Hindelanger Klettersteig.
The Wengenköpfe in the background.*

(Giebelhaus - Edmund-Probst-Haus). From here you can see the summit cross on the Grosser Daumen (2280m), and it will take you only 15-20mins gentle walk up the grassy dome to reach it. The superfit may wish to continue along the ridge to the summit of the Kleiner Daumen (2191m). The ridge begins wide but, after the pass where a track crosses (west to the Haseneckalpe and the Rettenschwangertal valley and east to the Engeratsgundsee lake), narrows considerably.

Descents
a) From the Grosser Daumen return to the flat depression with the signpost to the Giebelhaus and the Edmund-Probst-Haus huts, then follow the truly idyllic path past the tranquil tarns and back to the upper station of the Nebelhorn cableway. (Last descent to Oberstdorf at 1700.)
b) Starting from the pass between the Grosser Daumen and the Kleiner Daumen, take the track to the west through the high meadows of the Haseneckalmen and down into the Rettenschwangtal valley. Then follow the roadway (no motor vehicles allowed) to Bad Oberdorf and Hindelang.
c) If you want to make a long day of it by adding the climbing path across the Hohe Gänge (Route 7), then take descent b) as far as the Upper Haseneckalm (1690m). A little way on, but before you reach the Middle Haseneckalm, take a narrow path to your right and clamber to the summit of the Rotspitze. Then follow Route 7.

Difficulty
Quite a demanding ridge route with some very exposed sections. Adequately protected but only where necessary. Requires considerable surefootedness and absolute freedom from vertigo. Good safety margins in sudden bad weather by reason of the three escape routes.

Altitude differences
Oberstdorf - Nebelhorn 1396m; Nebelhorn - Grosser Daumen 56m; many counter-climbs.

Climbing path length
c.5km, but remember the counter-climbs.

Times
Climbing path Nebelhorn - Grosser Daumen or vice versa, 3-3½hrs; from the Grosser Daumen back to the Koblatt by the walkers' path, 2½hrs; Grosser Daumen - Kleiner Daumen, c.¾hr.

Bases
Berghotel Höfatsblick (1929m) at the top cable car station. Edmund-Probst-Haus (1925m); service mid December to mid Oct. 60B, 60M.

KLETTERSTEIG

On the Hindelanger Klettersteig, Allgau Alps.

6. HOCHVOGEL 2593m
Allgäu Alps, Main Ridge

The Hochvogel is remarkable for its beautiful shape and for the wonderful views from the summit. The climbing path to the top - the Bäumenheimer Weg - is well waymarked and adequately, though not everywhere, protected. Breathtaking views down into the Hornbachtal valley and magnificent rock scenery make it a rewarding outing for experienced walkers who are reasonably unaffected by vertigo. Combined with a descent via the Fuchskar it makes a rich and varied round trip.

Approach
Via Hinterhornbach (1101m) in the valley of the same name, which runs into the Lech valley. Drive via Reutte in Tirol (Austria), which in turn can be reached by the so-called Deutsche Alpenstrasse from Oberau through Ettal and past Linderhof, or via Garmisch-Partenkirchen and Lermoos.

Ascent to the Schwabegg hut (privately owned)
From the Gasthof Adler follow the prominent signboard pointing up to the nearby edge of the woods. The path continues through the wood for 15-20 mins to a fence. On this section take great care at one very exposed place. From the fence, cross some meadows to an old house (with a number plate, No.21). A few steps beyond, join a road for c50m, then branch off right at a signboard. (About here, if you are in luck, you may hear the Hinterhornbach carillon.) After a few minutes cross a wider, grassy, level track and follow the path for another 15-20 mins to another road. Take the road for about 250m, then turn right into the woods on a waymarked path and continue fairly steeply through woods, then Latschen, to the Schwabegg hut.

Summit ascent
From the hut, the path rises fairly steeply through Latschen. After ½-¾ hr, where the Latschen end, it flattens out and heads for the headland at the foot of the north-east ridge, where the climbing path leaves the normal path (1977m). If you are going to take the climbing path, it is, of course, best to use it for the ascent, so traverse left into the Rosskar and savour the superb views to the south as you cross the combe on more or less level ground.

When you reach the west ridge the path turns right, towards the rock, and leads into a scree gully running down from the east buttress.

KLETTERSTEIG

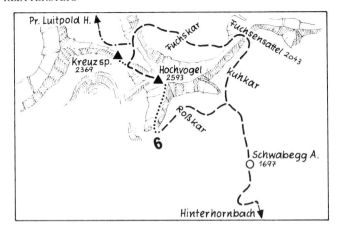

(Beware of rock falls.) The route soon escapes to the right, onto the buttress to the east, and up to a secondary ridge above the head of the gully. Now go right again to the next massive buttress and follow the waymarks (and enough wire ropes for safety) over ledges and gullies to the summit rocks. Just before the summit, go left into a scree-filled cove and then, up a final wire rope, straight to the summit cross.

Descent
Follow the waymarks down the north-east ridge over some rock steps, and then down a series of hairpins, in part over broken rock and scree. Next the path goes along a broad ledge, called the Schnur (= string or cord), which swings round the south-west shoulder under a rock overhang and offers a quick, unexpected panoramic view before it reaches the gap just a little further on. You may feel tempted to make the short, partly protected, diversion up onto the Kreuzspitze (2369m) - from where there are routes to the Prinz-Luitpold-Haus (hut). Back at the gap, take the path down the east side into the wide Fuchskar combe, then over broken rock and snow fields in amongst the shattered boulders of the Salzboden (c.1890m). Now the route climbs through crags, gaining about 150m of altitude, to the Fuchsensattel (2043m) - the gap between the Hochvogel and the Rosszahn group - before descending into the well-watered Kuhkar. After another rise of c.55m it comes to full circle, back to the junction with the Bäumenheimer Weg, and from there returns to Hinterhornbach down the ascent route.

Difficulty
The complete round trip requires considerable stamina. The climbing path section additionally demands freedom from vertigo and surefootedness. In the higher sections there is serious risk of rock falls. Some climbing Grade I. A very long day tour.

Times
Hinterhornbach - Bäumenheimer Weg - Hochvogel, 4-5 hrs; Hochvogel - Fuchskarsattel - Hinterhornbach 3½-4½ hrs.

Bases
If required or desired, Prinz-Luitpold-Haus (1846m); service Whitsun - mid-Oct; 25B, 139M, 44L. Schwabegg hut (private); service; no overnight facilities.

Altitude differences
Hinterhornbach - Hochvogel 1492m; Prinz-Luitpold-Haus - Hochvogel 747m.

Climbing path altitude
c.500m.

7. ROTSPITZE 2033m AND BREITENBERG 1887m
Allgäu Alps, Daumen group (see map p. 30)

This fairly harmless but varied climbing path along the Hohe Gänge (High Passage) - the wild and jagged ridge connecting the Rotspitze to the Breitenberg - was equipped in 1973. It used to be an easy climbers' route, but it can now be warmly recommended as an entertaining day's outing to all climbing-path enthusiasts, even novices.

The 3½km ridge has been protected with one steel rung and about 200m of wire rope. There are no waymarks. The original steel ropes were plastic covered, but they proved unsuitable and had to be replaced after only a year by the present, normal wire ropes.

Approach
The best route up the Rotspitze starts at Bruck im Ostrachtal (860m), which lies at the end of a narrow metalled road from Hindelang. From Munich the way to Hindelang is via Garmisch and Reutte, or by the shorter route via Ettal and Linderhof. From Augsburg take the B17, from Ulm the B19.

Ascent of the Rotspitze
300m south of the tiny hamlet of Bruck, by the power station and the monument to Luitpold, the Bavarian Prince Regent, cross the bridge and turn right at the signpost marked 'Retterschwangtal', on a track which soon turns into a forest path (no waymarks). Follow it for about

KLETTERSTEIG

¾ hr to a track, then follow the track for about 10 mins to a signboard - where your route is joined by the much less enjoyable approach from the Hornkapelle near Bruck. Now turn left and climb for about 1 hr up a waymarked, but steep and exhausting path, through the upper forest to a fork at the Häbelesgundalp. The left-hand path goes to the Breitenberg, the right-hand one to the Rotspitze; so this is where you will complete your circuit. The path to the Rotspitze now climbs in a series of hairpins to the saddle cut into the north ridge to the right of the summit, then more pleasantly on wire ropes over rock and grass up to the summit cross.

Ridge route
Follow the waymarked track south-east from the summit to the signboard 'Retschenschwanger Tal - Haseneck' in the first gap. Here continue left along the ridge on an unmarked track over grass and easy crags onto the Heubatspitze (2002m). The ridge now turns north, and this is where the climbing path proper begins. A series of wire ropes takes you along a delightful sequence of ups and downs, alternating between the left and right flanks of the ridge. To your left the view is down onto the shattered boulders of the Häbelesgrund combe, to your right onto the green meadows of the Elpenalpe. This entertaining scramble ends - all too soon - at the edge of the Latschen that cover the top of the Breitenberg, and about 30 mins easy walk from the summit.

Descent
From the Breitenberg take the waymarked track down to the Elpenalpe (1309m; sometimes fresh milk for sale), and then down to the valley floor by a shady path through the woods. At the signpost at the edge of the wood, follow the sign 'Oibelesweg-Haidachringweg' over idyllic meadows first on the western, then the eastern bank of the Ostrach, and back to your starting point. Only the last few minutes, after the weir, will involve walking a metalled road.

Difficulty
Day trip: recommended for beginners, provided they are reasonably fit and moderately footsure and free from vertigo.

Times
Bruck - Rotspitze 2½-3 hrs; Rotspitze - Breitenberg 1½-2 hrs; Breitenberg - Bruck 2-2½ hrs (or 3-3½ hrs if ascending).

Bases
None.

Altitude difference
Bruck - Rotspitze 1173m.
Length of climbing path
c.3½ km.
Note
The climbing path from the Breitenberg to the Nebelhorn is the Hindelanger Klettersteig (see Route 5).

8. ROTE FLÜH 2111m AND SCHARTSCHROFEN 1973m
Allgäu Alps, Tannheim Mountains

The Rote Flüh is the westernmost peak of the horseshoe round the Reintal valley which forms the main group of the Tannheim Mountains. The way over the summit, from the Judenscharte to the Gelbe Scharte *(or vice versa)* via two enjoyable climbing paths, is a favourite tour in this region. In 1974 another climbing path, the Friedberger Steig, was installed on the Schartschrofen immediately to the west of the Gelbe Scharte gap. It is little known and short, but a real classic. It can be taken as a tasty dessert after the Rote Flüh crossing; it also allows assured non-vertigo-sufferers to make the direct passage from the Füssener Jöchl pass onto the Gimpel (2160m) via Schartschrofen, Gelbe Scharte, Rote Flüh and Judenscharte, which was previously the preserve of advanced climbers because of the difficult pitches on the south face of the Schartschrofen.

Approach
From Nesselwängle (1047m), which lies in the Tannheim valley, about half-way between Weissenbach and Tannheim and a little east of the serene Haldensee lake.

Ascent to the Gimpelhaus (hut)
Start at the sign at the west end of the churchyard. (Note that the hut has its own car park just above the churchyard and to the left.) Follow the road a few yards up, to the Hotel Berghof, and then a few more yards to the right, to a signboard. Now follow the fence to the first waymark on stones in the meadow. The steep path hairpins up through the woods to the Gimpelhaus (1720m). The present huge building replaced the old hut, which burnt down in 1973.

Summit Ascent
The path is easily missed where it begins again beyond the hut. It goes

KLETTERSTEIG

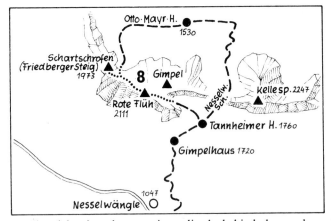

up to the right, i.e. the east, immediately behind the north-west corner of the long *alm* buildings.

Do not take the path to the left: it leads to the climbers' pitches on the south wall of the Rote Flüh. The correct path rises through Latschen and meadows, first in hairpins, then in a sweeping left-hand curve. It meets a path from the Tannheim hut, passes under the south wall of the Gimpel, rises to the Judenscharte gap and finally reaches the summit of the Rote Flüh by a harmless little 15 mins climbing path.

Descent

Start down the south-west ridge on the zig-zagging wire ropes, then traverse a section of vertical wall on steel-peg footholds. A little further on the route crosses to the north-west ridge, then easily traverses round the south face of the Gilmenkopf on wire ropes to reach the Gelbe Scharte (½-¾hr). Here the sign 'Friedberger Steig -nur für Geübte ('...experienced scramblers only') beckons towards a diversion up 200m of wire ropes onto the Schartschrofen. The route first bears right, to by-pass the first steep tower, then continues up over steep grass and crags on the left of the ridge. The next section is wild and, in places, extremely exposed, and leads up to a narrow gully - almost a chimney - in which you climb to the summit. This used to be a true Grade II climb. Today any scramblers who enjoy real freedom from vertigo will experience 40 mins. of pure pleasure, heightened by the magnificent views of the mighty north-face cliffs of the Gimpel and the Rote Flüh.

ALLGÄU ALPS ROUTE 8

Back at the Gelbe Scharte, the main route goes down steeply to the Otto Mayr hut in the Reintal. This is the valley which runs from the great horseshoe of rock walls in the west down the centre of the Tannheim group. From the hut, the path climbs steeply once more to the Nesselwängler Scharte - the pass between the Schäfer and the Kellespitze. The summit of the Kellespitze (2247m) is a 1hr. Grade I climb from the pass. Our path goes straight down from the pass, past the Tannheim hut and the Gimpelhaus, back to Nesselwängle.

Difficulty
Easy one-day tour; some degree of freedom from vertigo required for the descent from the Rote Flüh to the Gelbe Scharte; but the short Friedberger Steig demands scrambling skills of somewhat higher order.

Times
Nesselwängle - Gimpelhaus 1½hrs; Gimpelhaus - Rote Flüh 1-1¼hrs; Rote Flüh - Gelbe Scharte ½-¾hr. (or 1 hr. for ascent); detour to Schartschrofen ½-¾hr; Gelbe Scharte - Otto Mayr hut 2hrs; Otto Mayr hut - Nesselwängle 2hrs.

Bases
Gimpelhaus (1720m); 40B, 100M. Otto Mayr hut (1530m); service end May-end Oct, plus Christmas, Easter and Whitsun; 27B, 30M, 10L. (immediately next door) Willi Merkl memorial hut (1550m); 30L; key from Friedberg group of the Augsburg section of the DAV (German Alpine Club). New Füssen hut (1535m); service end May-end Oct; 61L. Tannheim hut (1760m); warden mid May-end Sept; self-catering; 25M.

Altitude differences
Nesselwängle - Gimpelhaus 673m; Gimpelhaus - Rote Flüh 391m; Rote Flüh - Otto Mayr hut 581m; Otto Mayr hut - Nesselwängler Scharte 477m.

Climbing path altitudes
Judenscharte - Rote Flüh c.140m; Gelbe Scharte - Rote Flüh 210m; Friedberger Steig c.70m.

KLETTERSTEIG

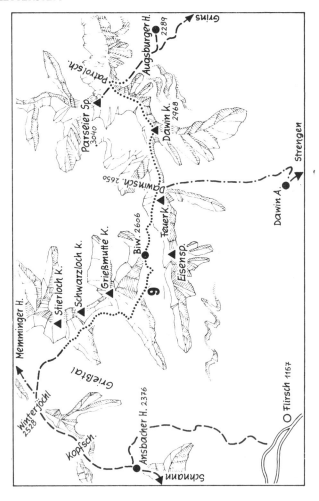

Lechtal Alps

9. AUGSBURGER HÖHENWEG AND PARSEIERSPITZE 3040m.

The direct route between the Augsburg hut and the Ansbach hut -called the Augsburger Höhenweg (= high-level route) - is the jewel of the Lechtal Alps, and indeed one of the most magnificent high-altitude routes anywhere in the northern limestone Alps. An extra bonus is that only a short detour at the start or finish of the tour is needed to take in the Parseierspitze, the highest peak of the whole northern range. This is a demanding alpine excursion, not only because of its great length, but more particularly because it includes snow-fields and ice-couloirs, and sections liable to rock-fall. In thunderstorms, high winds or snowstorms these dangers can become grave. If conditions become tricky, the wire-rope protection and the bivouac-box can prove to be life-savers.

Approaches
a) From Grins (1015m), above Pians (856m).
b) From Flirsch (1157m).
c) From Schnann (1180m).
These villages are all in the Stanz valley between St. Anton am Arlberg and Landeck (railway station).

Ascents to the Augsburg hut
The hut, on its wonderful site below the Gatschkopf, is visible from the valley. The waymarked path starts at the last parking place above Grins, near the swimming pool, and climbs steeply for 3-4hrs. The old centre of Grins is perfectly preserved, and the wrought-iron cross in front of the church is one of the finest anywhere in the Alps.

Ascents to the Ansbach hut
a) From Flirsch take a steep waymarked path through the upper reaches of the forest and then over expansive meadows to reach the hut in 3-4hrs.
b) From Schnann take an equally steep and rather awkward path via the Fritz hut (1800m) in 3½hrs.

KLETTERSTEIG

The Höhenweg
From the Augsburg hut retrace your ascent route a little way, as far as the depression below the Gasillschlucht ravine. Follow unclear tracks up an exhausting slope to the foot of the rock face, then take the wire ropes and steel rungs into the ravine itself. The protection continues, and the route soon escapes to the right onto wide, level, friendlier rock ledges to reach the gap below the Parseierspitze. (For the summit ascent, see the separate section below.)

Next traverse a snow-field (with special care over the first section, which will be wet and slippery) and climb up wire ropes to a gap. Now cross the craggy ridge to the south flank and take to the wire rope for the very exposed ascent onto the Dawinkopf, which, at 2968m, is the highest peak on the ridge and the third highest of any in the northern limestone Alps. Descend down the north ridge, which is only partly protected and sometimes covered in ice; then follow the wire ropes across a vast snow-field and onto the south flank of the Oberer Schwarze Kopf. Next a splendid but simple rock traverse will present you with some fine views and take you onto the broad, even ridge that leads down to the Dawinscharte pass (2650m). (This is also the start of the only advisable emergency descent, an unmarked and not always very clear track going south down to Strengen and Grins.)

The menacing cliffs ahead are the buttresses of the Eisenkopf and Feuerkopf, and the next section, which traverses their steep north faces, is the most dangerous part of the route, with unsound rock, steep ice-couloirs, snow-fields and possible rock falls. Start along a narrow, slippery ledge (only partly protected) which slopes gently down to a welcome spring. Beside it on the rock is a memorial tablet which will help you not to forget the very real danger of rock-falls at this point. The route now climbs again, over the flank of a rock spur projecting from the north face, and up into the Gelbes Schartl gap, beyond which there is, once more, grave danger of rock-falls. The route goes down some steep wire ropes into a very steep ice-couloir, which you must cross. This can be a tricky spot, and you should make the crossing either with the aid of an ice-axe or on a rope properly belayed. Continue down an innocuous snow-field, cross the depression, then climb again in hairpins up steep but harmless crags, and cross a second, steeper combe over loose and wet, but easy ground to reach the Parseierscharte (2606m). Here you will be surprised to come upon the smart, modern Augsburg bivouac-box, which was flown in here by helicopter in 1976. There is a possible emergency descent southwards from the pass, but I strongly advise against it because its lower sections run through rough terrain crossed by ravines, and are very hard to find.

The worst is now over and the rest of the route is, by comparison, a mere stroll. From the bivouac go south, down into the combe, then, slightly right, across to the grass shoulder. Now continue in a sweeping curve round the boulder-strewn south-west flank, then take an easy, almost level, rock ledge across the tumultuous and sometimes very swollen torrents rushing down the faces of the Grossmuttekopf, the Schwarzlochkopf and the Stierlochkopf. At the end of the ledge a scree gully leads down to a snow-field. Continue down over a spur of broken rock, then up to a little gap and down again, in the bottom of another scree gully. Now a comfortable path leads down to the top of the Griestal valley - which, if you are interested in fauna, has a flourishing population of marmots - where the climbing path proper finally and manifestly ends. Continue to the Winterjöchl (2528m) and at the junction either turn right for the Memmingen hut or join long-distance path No. 601 to walk gently up and down via the Kopfscharte (2484m) to the Ansbach hut.

Ascent of the Parseierspitze
Gluttons for punishment will want to bag the Parseierspitze (3040m) at the beginning or end of their tour.
a) The south-east wall, which rises 200m out of the permanent snow of the Grinner Ferner, can be climbed up a flank of crag and loose rock. From near the eastern end follow faded waymarks over rock steps and fallen boulders, more or less directly towards the summit but bearing slightly left about halfway up the face. (c.1hr; Grade II; liable to rock-falls; ropes advisable.)
b) The east ridge avoids the danger from falling rocks, but is a good deal more difficult. Enter the ridge from the permanent snow in the Patrolscharte gap (2844m) and traverse to the right round the first, slightly overhanging pinnacle. The middle section is Grade III and ropes are essential.

Variant over the Gatschkopf
Summit-baggers who want to avoid the difficult section of the climbing path through the Gasillschlucht may prefer the easier alternative over the summit of the Gatschkopf (2947m). This is the peak directly behind the Augsburg hut. From one side it looks no more than a great mound of loose rock, but the north side plunges down dangerous precipices. A waymarked path will take you from the hut to the top in 1½ hrs, or from the Patrolscharte in a few minutes. But keep off the dangerous east ridge!

KLETTERSTEIG

Descent
As ascent.

Difficulty
This high alpine route is to be taken very seriously. It requires total sure-footedness, considerable freedom from vertigo and much stamina. It is no day excursion! Unsuitable for children. In poor weather the problems multiply. In snow, take ropes, ice-axe and perhaps crampons. Grave danger of rock-falls in some sections. Parseierspitze: Grade II via south-east face, or Grades II and III via east ridge (ropes essential). Gatschkopf: simple.

Times
Grins - Augsburg hut 3-4 hrs (descent 2-3 hrs); Flirsch - Ansbach hut 3-4 hrs (descent 2-3 hrs); Schnann - Ansbach hut c.3½ hrs (descent c.2½ hrs); Augsburger Höhenweg, in either direction, 8-10 hrs.

Bases
Augsburg hut (2289m); service early July - early Sept; 16B, 24M, 10L: Ansbach hut (2376m); services early July - mid-Sept; 8B, 40M, 8L. Augsburg bivouac-box (2606m); 4L.

Altitude difference
Grins - Augsburg hut 1274m; Flirsch - Ansback hut 1219m; Schann - Ansbach hut 1196m; Augsburg hut - Parseierspitze 751m.

Climbing path length
c.20km from hut to hut!

Wetterstein

10. ALPSPITZE 2629m
Wetterstein, Blassenkamm ridge

The ascent of the Alpspitze by way of the Schöne Gänge *(lovely passage)* is one of the best-loved and most trodden of all German mountain tours. Connoisseurs can make a gourmet outing of it by continuing with a descent down the wire ropes into the Mathaisenkar, while novices who have found the excitements of the climbing path to the summit quite sufficient can come down by the easy path via the south-west ridge and the Stuibensee. I would advise against making the tour in the opposite direction - i.e. from Hammersbach up the Höllental and through the Mathaisenkar - except perhaps for those endowed with exceptional stamina.

Approaches
Leave Garmisch by the Ehrwald road (B24). At the edge of the town a left fork leads to the lower stations of the Kreuzeck and Osterfelderkopf cableways. The best approach is to take one or other of them to the top.

Summit ascents
a) From Kreuzeck (1652m) take the path to the Hochalm (1705m). (c.½ hr; fine views.) Continue uphill to the Hochalmsattel, and then into the combe at the foot of the Bermardeinwände face. Climb, over some rubble and a scree run, to the base of the rocks following the waymarks and a few wire ropes westwards to the foot of the Schöne Gänge. The next section is exposed, but interesting and much easier than it appears. It leads up some well-secured steel rungs and some thick wire ropes south-west to the grassy saddle at the top of the Bernardeinwände, and then into the Oberkar. The path which joins here from the east has come up an easier way (which, however, takes 1 hr longer) via the Bernardein hut and the Stuibenwald.

From the Oberkar follow the waymarks as they go quite steeply up the Schulter *(shoulder)* and onto the east ridge. Now either continue on the waymarks up the north flank of the ridge, or take an unmarked and more exposed, but much more interesting, route up the actual edge of the ridge. Both alternatives are easy, command fine views and soon take you to the summit.

b) Another possibility is to go right before reaching the Schulter and struggle up the waymarked path over the screes of the gigantic Ostkar combe. This is certainly not recommended for climbing path enthusiasts in normal conditions, but it is the best and safest descent in bad visibility.

c) You can save yourself 300m and about 1 hr of steep walking by riding up the Osterfelderkopf cableway (upper station 2033m) and then climbing the Nordwandsteig up the north face. It will take you first through two short man-made tunnels through the rock, then onto an artificially-widened rock ledge with a fine view. Now climb some easy steel pegs and a long, gently-angled ladder to gain the remaining bit of height to the Oberkar, and continue as at a) or (b above.

d) In 1978 a new climbing path was opened - called the Alpspitz-Ferrata - up the west side of the broad expanse of the north wall of the Alpspitze, to give scramblers over the Alpspitze an alternative to the Nordwandsteig. This is now far and away the most attractive ascent on the north side, and it has, not surprisingly, been hugely popular since the day it first opened.

From the upper station of the Osterfelderkopf cableway, start south along the Nordwandsteig route, along the foot of the Höllentorkopf. The new Alpspitz-Ferrata branches off at a sign about 100m beyond the sharp outline of the pinnacle. The lower part of the new route follows the old climbers' path to the north-wall climbs. Follow a pathway to the foot of the first buttress, then climb a series of ladders up crags. At the top our route leaves the climbers' path to head west into the Stoa'rösl-Scharte gully. Stop for a moment to admire the spectacular views across the Zugspitze group and the Höllentalferner glacier, then continue up a succession of couloirs and crags until you are level with the *Herzel*. Now, as the route gets considerably steeper, follow the excellent protection up the north face across a sheer but well protected buttress, and onto the north-west ridge of the Alpspitze. The ridge leads you to the foot of the final summit approach, where the route goes along a natural terrace round to the west slopes. For the final scramble to the summit, follow the excellent protection up a steep couloir - but beware of rock falls. A little below the summit couloir, there is some wire rope leading round the western side of the summit rocks onto the south ridge, and a project is afoot to install proper protection from this point to the summit.

Descent

If the weather is good, experienced and reasonably skilful scramblers in search of new experiences may like to try the very rewarding, protected descent into the Mathaisenkar. The first section is a 30 mins simple (Grade I) climb on wire ropes down the south-west ridge. There is an alternative descent from the first gap, the Grieskarscharte (2430m), eastwards by an unmarked and intermittent track into the Grieskar combe and back to the Kreuzeck via the Stuibensee and the Bernardein hut. But the climbing path into the Mathaisenkar, adequately protected and crossing magnificent terrain, branches right shortly before you get all the way down into the gap. Start down a c.50m drop through a rather steep gully, then double back left over slanting slabs at the foot of a rock step. If the wire ropes in this section are under remnants of winter snow, as they often are in early summer, then you must not attempt to traverse this very slippery shelf except properly roped and belayed. Otherwise turn round and make the alternative descent into the Grieskar mentioned above. Beyond the slab shelf, well-placed wire ropes will take you down in a north-westerly direction and then across the western flank of the ridge through some magnificent landscape. From the bottom of the wire ropes go south-west to a memorial plaque, and continue down into the combe on a barely discernable track with only occasional waymarks, over a mixture of broken rock and grass. This section, from the bottom of the wire ropes to the combe, is very difficult to navigate in bad visibility. Once in the combe, turn west on a rather indistinct path over broken rock (or sometimes old snow) to join a much clearer path which goes, more or less level, through a belt of Latschen, then sweeps round the side of a grassy, conical knoll. At about 1600m turn sharp left (west) and down, first in steep hairpins, then slanting down through mixed wood, until you see the Höllentalanger hut just ahead. From the hut simply walk down the Höllentalklamm valley to Hammersbach. (For a description of this section, see ascent in Route 12 below.)

Difficulty

Kreuzeck - Alpenspitze and back, easy day excursion. Adding descent into Mathaisenkar makes a more strenuous tour, which becomes very strenuous if undertaken in the opposite direction - i.e. starting from Hammersbach. Schöne Gänge and descent into Mathaisenkar require surefootedness and freedom from vertigo. In poor visibility Mathaisenkar requires very good route-finding skills.

The bent rungs at the start of the Alpspitz-Ferrata.

Times
Kreuzeck - Alpenspitze 3-4 hrs; Osterfelderkopf - Alpenspitze 2½-3½ hrs; Alpenspitze - Mathaisenkar - Hammersbach 4-5 hrs; Alpenspitze - Stuibensee - Kreuzeck 3-4 hrs; Hammersbach - Höllentalanger hut - Mathaisenkar - Alpspitze 6-7 hrs.

Bases
Adolf-Zoeppritz-Haus (hut), at Kreuzeck (1652m); service all year 61B, 74M, 10L: Hochalm (1705m service all year; 7B, 30M. Höllentalanger hut (1381m): service early June - mid-Oct; 2B, 90M, 20L: winter shelter with 16M. Knappenhäuser (hut) (1527m); summer service; 6B, 25M. Kreuzjochhaus (1600m); 39B, 88M, 5 min from Kreuzeckhaus.

Altitude differences
Garmisch - Alpspitze and Hammersbach - Alpspitze, both c.1900m; Kreuzeck - Alpspitze 980m; Osterfelderkopf - Alspitze 809m.

Climbing path altitudes
Schöne Gänge c.200m; Norwandsteig (length) c.500m; Alpspitze - Grieskarscharte 164m; Mathaisenkar c.668m.

11. RIFFELSCHARTE 2161m
Wetterstein, Riffelwand ridge

The climbing path section on the Riffelscharte crossing is rather short compared with those on offer on the nearby Zugspitze and Alpspitze. It just runs from the Riffelriss combe across the west wall and up to the gap, so experienced scramblers will probably consider it only as a possible substitute tour for occasions when the Zugspitze or the Mathaisenkar are ruled out by the time of year (too much snow, old or new) or by uncertain weather. But it makes an excellent outing for beginners, with a magnificent panorama of the whole Zugspitze group and plunging views down to the Eibsee as extra attractions.

Approaches
a) From Hammersbach (see Route 12).
b) From Garmisch, drive out on the Ehrwald road (B24) to c.1½km beyond the edge of the town. 300m beyond the turning to Hammersbach, fork left to the Eibsee and from there take the German Zugspitze railway to the Riffelriss station (1685m).

Ascent to the Höllentalanger hut
See Route 12

KLETTERSTEIG

The Riffelscharte (centre) separates the Waxensteinkamm (right) from the Riffelwandkamm (left). The Höllental in the foreground.
a) Höllental - Riffelscharte Route 11. b) Höllental - Zugspitze Route 12.

Summit ascents
a) The best route starts at the Höllentalanger hut and follows Route 12 to the very head of the Höllental valley, where the paths to the Zugspitze and the Riffelscharte divide. Take the right fork and follow the waymarks (rather widely spaced at first), steeply up the eastern slopes across rocks and some Latschen. Continue on wire ropes up a short, steep gully, and then up a second protected, but less steep, section into the grassy lower depression of the Riffelkar combe. (From here to the top the route may be difficult to find in mist.) At a point where an indistinct path branches off to the right (the Schafsteig to the Waxenstein ridge), our route turns sharp left across broken rock and scree, climbs to the upper depression of the combe and continues below the Riffelkopf up to the Riffelscharte gap. If the weather is clear, then detours to the summits of the Riffeltorkopf (left) or the Southern Riffelspitze (right) are quick, easy and very rewarding.
b) As described under descents a) or b) below.

Descents
From the gap go a few yards left and uphill, round the north side of the Rittertorkopf to where the wire ropes begin. Now enjoy about 20 mins of stupendous views down onto the Eibsee as you scramble down the well-protected climbing path over rather exposed slabs into the gigantic, boulder-strewn Riffelriss combe. From here there is a choice.
a) From the foot of the rock face follow an indistinct track down and left over scree, then onto a grassy tongue where a path continues down to the Riffelriss station of the Zugspitze railway. Now the path gets wider and leads down left to the so-called Grenzgasse (= frontier lane - because it runs down the line of the German-Austrian border), where it joins the path from the Wiener Neustadt hut and then follows a ski piste down to Eibsee.
b) Take the old Riffelscharte path down the Riffelreisse screes to the funicular tracks. Cross near the lower entrance of a little tunnel and walk down through woods and finally over the meadows called Am Wasserbühel to the Eibsee.

From the Eibsee to Hammersbach, either take the train or walk along the so-called Unterer Nordsteig - a lovely wooded path, but a bit difficult to follow as some of the forks and junctions are not waymarked.

KLETTERSTEIG

Difficulty
Moderately strenuous day excursion. Surefootedness and freedom from vertigo required on the climbing path sections. Mist or snow can make route-finding difficult on the upper half of the ascent on the east side.

Times
Hammersbach - Höllentalanger hut 2-2½ hrs; Höllentalanger hut -Riffelscharte 2-2½ hrs; Eibsee - Hammersbach via Unterer Nordsteig 2-3 hrs; Or from west to east: Eibsee - Riffelriss 1½ hrs; Riffelriss - Riffelscharte 1½-2 hrs.

Base
Höllentalanger hut (1381m); service early June - mid-Oct; 2B, 90M, 20L: winter shelter with 16M.

Altitude differences
Hammersbach - Riffelscharte 1390m; Eibsee - Riffelscharte 1190m; Riffelriss station - Riffelscharte 416m.

Climbing path altitude
c.200m.

12. ZUGSPITZE 2963m VIA HÖLLENTAL
Wetterstein, principal summit

The Zugspitze is the highest peak in Germany, and of all the high peaks of the Alps it is probably the most frequented, the easiest of mechanical access and, alas, the most spoiled. But, along with all these negative superlatives, there is also a positive one for climbing path enthusiasts. The ascent from the top of the Höllentalferner glacier to the summit and the section lower down over the rock faces at the so-called Leiter (ladder) and the Brett (plank), add up to the longest continuous artificially protected climbing path in the whole northern limestone Alps. It certainly bears comparison with many of the classic *via ferrata* routes in the Dolomites. It requires exceptional stamina and fitness to complete the excursion in a single day, so I would advise the average scrambler to plan a night stop at the Höllentalanger hut. Finally, if you want to experience just about every possible kind of climbing-path pleasure to be had in the northern limestone Alps, then combine this ascent with a descent via the Wiener Neustadt hut (see Route 13).

Approach
Leave Garmisch by the Ehrwald road (B24). About 1 km beyond the edge of the town turn left and drive 2 km along a narrow, winding road to Hammersbach (753m). Try the little car park just before the

WETTERSTEIN ROUTE 12

The Höllental route up the Zugspitze.

KLETTERSTEIG

bridge over the Hammersbach stream; if this is full, drive back to the larger car park 400m further back.

Ascent to the Höllentalanger hut
a) Take the dirt road between the stream and the little chapel. It starts flat, but after the next bridge turns right and climbs steeply in the shade of tall trees to the lower station of a little goods cableway. A few steep hairpins on a good footpath take you up to the Höllentalklamm hut (¾-1 hr; admission charge, but Alpine Club members free).

  The next half hour is an experience in itself, as the route goes through the Höllentalklamm gorge. You will walk for 1 km wrapped in gloom and assailed by the splash and roar of white water (but protected from rock-falls and avalanches) on a path which has been cut through the gorge, mainly through tunnels blasted through solid rock. (Electric lighting 7.00 to 19.00. Be careful when descending: the rock and the wooden bridges are always wet and slippery.) The intermittent views are breathtaking - all plunging water and remnants of avalanches as tall as houses. When you finally re-emerge into the daylight, the path leads up in steep zig-zags to the Höllentalanger hut (c.1hr). (It is possible to detour round the gorge by taking the Stangensteig path just before the start of the gorge, on which you will end by crossing a daring bridge and looking down nearly 75m into the stream below.)

b) Even late risers and tardy starters can get to the Höllentalanger hut fresh and at a reasonable hour by taking the Osterfelderkopf cableway (see Route 10 for approach). From the Osterfelderkopf (2033m) walk downhill a little way, then up again to the Hupfleitenjoch. Now the path goes downhill again, through magnificent scenery above the Höllentalklamm, past the Knappenhäuser (hut) to the Höllentalanger hut. If you catch the first gondola (at 8.00) you will reach the hut by 9.00, but of course by then those who stayed overnight are likely to be well on their way up, 2-3 hrs ahead.

c) If you do not fancy the uphill section of b) above, there is an alternative from the Osterfelderkopf: the Rinderschartensteig, an old track recently restored into a wide tourist path, which runs down the west slope to join b) above just before the hut.

Summit ascent
From the Höllentalanger hut first cross the stream to the right, then

follow a gently-uphill path to the fork at the very top of the valley (½ hr). Look out for the sign and the waymarks, pointing right for the Riffelscharte, left for the Zugspitze. The left-hand route soon reaches the first wire ropes and then the Leiter, which consists of a series of steel rungs climbing almost vertically up a 20m rock step. Continue on the wire ropes to the Brett, one of the most exposed sections on the route, where steel pegs and wire ropes make a horizontal traverse across a slab 40m wide and sloping at about 55°. The next section climbs, clear and well marked, into the Höllentalkar and up to the Grüner Buckel (green hump). Continue upwards over moraine to the scree-covered lower section of the Höllentalferner. Go more or less up the middle of the snow-covered glacier (between crevasses to either side). Now climb some rather wobbly steel ladders up to a rock-strewn terrace which is your last chance of a comfortable rest before the summit. (If a thaw has made the bergschrund too wide where the path is supposed to cross, you can do so more conveniently a little higher.)

After your breather scramble up almost continuous wire ropes - all strong and well anchored - to the east summit of the Zugspitze (2-3 hrs). Continue towards the main summit, but about ½ hr before you reach it halt at the Irmerscharte gap, for your first view to the north into the Bayerisches Schneekar combe and onto the Eibsee far below. The final summit ascent can be quite tricky and requires extra care if, as is quite likely, and especially in early summer, there is old snow or ice on the rock.

Descents
a) As ascent (reckon 5-6 hrs).
b) To Ehrwald or Eibsee via the Wiener Neustadt hut (see Route 13; and don't forget to take your passport).
c) To Ehrwald via the Zugspitzgatterl. Take the protected path, or ride down on the cableway, to the Platt. Then walk down through the Zugspitzgatterl and the Ehrwald alm to Ehrwald (4-5 hrs) (see Route 15, ascent b); passports required).
d) To Garmisch from the Platt via the Knorr hut, the Reintal valley and the Partnachklamm gorge (6-8 hrs) (see Route 15, ascent a)).
e) To Eibsee, Garmisch, or Ehrwald (passports), by the Zugspitze railway or one of the two cableways.
f) As in Route 13 to the Wiener Neustadt hut and onto the Georg-Jäger-Stieg, but then branch right a little above the middle station of the cableway. Traverse the Ehrwalder Köpfe on a narrow path, then follow the wire ropes down an exposed buttress, and finally walk through the broken rock and Latschen

KLETTERSTEIG

to the Grenzgasse and on, down the Tunnelfenster ski-piste (tunnel window), to the Eibsee.

Difficulty
With a night stop at the Höllentalanger hut, pretty strenuous: without, herculean. Stamina, surefootedness, freedom from vertigo, some experience and at least a minimum of climbing skill are essential. Dangerous in bad weather, and especially in case of thunderstorms.

Times
Hammersbach - Höllentalanger hut 2-2½ hrs (or ½ hr longer via Stangensteig); Höllentalanger hut - summit 5-6 hrs.
Descents: Hammersbach via Höllentalanger hut 5-7 hrs; Ehrwald via Wiener Neustadt hut 3½-4½ hrs; Eibsee via Wiener Neustadt hut 4-5 hrs; Ehrwald via Zugspitzgatterl 4-5 hrs; Partnachklamm via Knorr hut 5-6 hrs.

Bases
Höllentalanger hut (1381m); service early June-mid Oct; 2B, 90M, 20L; winter shelter with 16M; telephone. Knappenhäuser (1527m); summer service; 6B, 25M. Klammeingang hut (1045m); snacks; no overnight facilities. Adolf-Zoeppritz-Haus (hut) (at the Kreuzeck) (1652m); service all year; 61B, 74M, 10L. Schneeferner-Haus (2650m); open all year; hotel and guest house with total of 100B; telephone. Münchner Haus (hut) (2962m); service mid-May-end Sept; 17M. Summit hotel of the Austrian cableway (2950m); restaurant, bar and accommodation; telephone. Summit station of the German railway and the German cableway; various buffets; telephone. Wiener Neustadt hut (2220m); summer service; 24B, 38M. Kreuzjockhaus (1600M), 5 min from Kreuzeckhaus, 39B, 88M.

Altitude differences
Hammersbach - Höllentalanger hut 630m; Höllentalanger hut - summit 1580m; Hammersbach - summit 2210m.

Climbing path altitudes
Leiter and Brett 110m; Höllentalferner - summit c.600m.

13. ZUGSPITZE 2963m   VIA WIENER NEUSTADT HUT
Wetterstein, main summit

This climbing path to the top of the Zugspitze is an alternative to the Höllental route. It is rather less exposed and, if you take the Austrian cableway up to the middle station, a great deal less strenuous without, however, lacking anything in natural grandeur. It is the better route in dubious weather conditions, not only because it is quicker, but also because the view is open towards the direction from which bad weather most often approaches. It is also recommended for those who lack that last edge of stamina.

WETTERSTEIN ROUTE 13

Approach
From Ehrwald turn north off the main road near the Lermoos/Garmisch junction and drive past the railway station about 3km to the lower station of the cableway at Obermoos.

Ascents to the Neustadt hut
It is best to take the cableway to the middle station (at pylon IV). There is a path up to this point - up the Bindersteig (which is partly a ski-piste) and the upper part of the Georg-Jäger-Steig (coming up from Ehrwald) - through Latschen and boulders to the Gamskar, but it is a 2-3 hrs walk and has little to recommend it.
From the Middle station:
a) Continue easily up the narrow Georg-Jäger-Steig to the Wiener Neustadt hut (½ hr).
b) If you are really surefooted and completely free from vertigo, you may like to try the climbing path directly up the ridge. It is very exposed, but wonderfully set into the mountain. This is not in fact an official climbing path, but simply a winter route between pylons IV and V for cableway maintenance, so before setting out, always enquire about its condition at the lower station or from cableway personnel. From the middle station follow the Georg-Jäger-Steig for a few minutes. Just before the path finally turns down northwards off the ridge you will see some rather ancient looking wire ropes hanging down from the first rock steps on your right. Follow them up onto the south side of the ridge, then climb a series of almost vertical ladders to pylon V, just above the Wiener Neustadt hut.

Summit ascent
From the hut walk up to the upper left-hand edge of the Österreichisches Schneekar (Austrian snow combe) to the beginning of the climbing path proper at the opening of the Stopzelzieher (a corkscrew), which is a wide natural tunnel going diagonally up through the rock like a chimney.

Once through this tunnel, continue upwards, first on steel rungs then on wire ropes, to the upper cableway station on the Zugspitzkamm (2805m) (2-2½ hrs). Now you can reach the main summit either by a second cableway or up another short climbing path to the left (½ hr). (Frontier-crossing. Remember your passports.)

Descents
See descents under Routes 12, 14 and 15.

KLETTERSTEIG

Difficulty
The climbing path between pylons IV and V requires absolute freedom from vertigo. Otherwise this is less demanding than the Höllental route.

Times
Lower station at Obermoos - middle station 2-3 hrs; middle station - Wiener Neustadt hut ½ hr; Wiener Neustadt hut - Zugspitzkamm 2-2½ hrs; Eibsee - Wiener Neustadt hut 4 hrs.

For times for descents, see Route 12.

Bases
Schneeferner-Haus (2650m); open all year; hotel and guest house with total of 100B; telephone. Münchner Haus (hut) (2957m); service early June-end-Sept; 17M. Summit hotel of the Austrian cableway (2950m); restaurant, bar and accommodation; telephone. Summit stations of the German railway and the German cableway; various buffets; telephone. Wiener Neustadt hut (2220m); summer service; 24B, 38M.

Altitude difference
Lower cableway station - Zugspitzkamm 1580m; lower station - Wiener Neustadt hut 995m; Zugspitzkamm - summit 158m.

Climbing path altitudes
Middle cableway station - pylon V c.200m; Stopselzieher - Zugspitzkamm c.550m.

14. SCHNEEFERNERKOPF 2875m
Wetterstein

The most impressive view of the Schneefernerkopf - with its characteristic flat, domed summit - is from Ehrwald. If it could be said to have a personality, it might be described as a quiet little sister to its noisy and more famous neighbour, the Zugspitze. Seen from the Zugspitzplatt, it stands out as one of the corner buttresses of the rim of rock enclosing the glacier. If the ascent to the summit is made from the Schneefernerscharte gap, and conditions are reasonable, then this is one of the shortest and easiest excursions in this book. If you start from the valley, then, of course, you will be taking on a long day's outing, but the climb to the Schneefernerkopf on the protected path up the north side can make a delightful addition to several other tours. You might like to add it to an ascent of the Zugspitze from Ehrwald, especially if you plan to return by the cableway; or enjoy it before a descent from the Zugspitze via the Gatterl or the Platt; or interpose it as a late afternoon filler between an ascent of the Zugspitze and an overnight stop at the Knorr hut.

WETTERSTEIN ROUTE 14

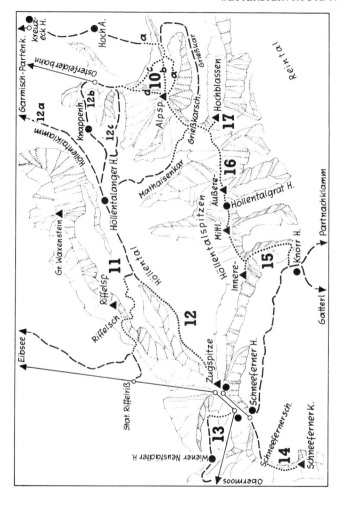

KLETTERSTEIG

The view of the south ridge of the Zugspitzecks from the ascent of the Schneefernerkopf.

WETTERSTEIN ROUTE 14

Ascent

Your first goal will be the Schneefernerscharte gap. To reach it from the Knorr hut or the Gatterl, make your way up the Platt by crossing the ski pistes and heading for the top of the highest of the ski-lifts. If your starting point was the summit of the Zugspitze or the upper station of the Austrian cableway - which also marks the top of the Wiener-Neustadt hut climbing path (see Route 13) - pick up the adequately protected and clearly defined route down the south face of the summit massif of the Zugspitze to the Schneefernerhaus (2650m) and then follow the obvious tracks through the snowfield. This section starts level, then climbs easily up to the Schneefernerscharte gap (2710m). Don't miss the spectacular view down the plunging precipices of the west face through the rock window nearby.

From the gap, scramble up some easy wire ropes, and up a few iron rungs at one or two steep rock steps, onto the broad shoulder. A few more minutes easy and almost level stroll will take you onto the expansive rock summit.

Descent

If you are sure that your experience and confidence are up to it and snow conditions are right, you may like to snow-run down one or other of the two steep snow couloirs which drop down from the shoulder of the ridge. But if you choose the more southerly of the two, be very careful at one dangerously narrow constriction.

For descents to the valley, see Routes 12 and 15.

Difficulty

The short ascent from the Schneefernerscharte gap is simple and follows a definite and well protected route. But the descent from the Zugspitze to the Schneefernerscharte is decidedly more testing and much longer.

Altitude differences

Lower station (Obermoos) of the Austrian cableway - Schneefernerkopf 1648m; Schneefernerhaus - Schneefernerkopf 185m

Climbing path altitude

c.150m

Times

Schneefernerhaus - Schneefernerkopf 1hr

Bases

Routes 12, 13 and 15

KLETTERSTEIG

15. INNERE HÖLLENTALSPITZE 2737m
Wetterstein, Blassenkamm ridge

For those who think that the western part of the famous Jubiläumsweg route - which includes some quite tricky bits of climbing - may be beyond their powers, there is a climbing path which will take them straight up to the protected part of the route. It begins at the Knorr hut and climbs up the south ridge of the Innere Höllentalspitze from the Brunntalkopf to the summit, where it meets the Jubiläumsweg.

Besides being an excellent excursion in its own right, it is also an easy way to reach the bivouac box on the Höllentalgrat ridge. But, more than that, it allows non-climbers to get a good taste of one of the most spectacular rock routes of the northern limestone Alps, on a section which also offers the reassurance of a variety of possible descents. Add a detour onto the Hochblassen, or the ridge route over the Alpspitze, and you have a wealth of choice including day tours and weekend excursions, with or without help from cableways, huts and bivouacs, and all well within the capacity of climbing path enthusiasts.

Approaches
a) From Garmisch via the Partnachklamm gorge.
b) From Ehrwald via the Ehrwald alm (by chair-lift if you prefer).
c) From Ehrwald via Obermoos and the cableway onto the Zugspitze (see Route 13).

Ascents to the Knorr hut
a) The normal ascent to the Knorr hut goes through the much-visited and truly astonishing Partnachklamm gorge, and then follows the new and rather dreary forest road into the Reintal valley. You can cut off one zig-zag (near the confluence with the Bodenlahn stream) by branching right onto the old track. Finally the road narrows to a footpath which will take you in c.3 hrs to the Bockhütte (standing just beyond the fork, where a path branches left to the Upper Reintal and the Schachen). 30 mins further up the valley, in wild, romantic scenery at the foot of the formidable north walls of the Jungfernkarkopf and the Hochwanner, the route passes some tarns called the Blaue Gumpen and then climbs along the northern slopes towards the Talriegel, where the Partnach hurls itself over the edge in a thunderous waterfall. I recommend the short detour to the actual falls; you will certainly not regret it. Above the falls continue

An exposed pitch on the Inneren Höllentalspitze.

through woods and across two avalanche tracks to the Reintalanger hut (1366m) (5-5½ hrs total so far). Now go on up the left bank of the Partnach. (A 15 mins detour on the right bank will take you to where the river gushes out of a rock cleft at its source.) The main route climbs in zig-zags up into the Brunntal and, past an open shelter, to a fork. Here either go right, through Latshchen and up across a huge sandy scree run, or, more comfortably, left along the floor of the Brunntal and then up the steep northern rim. The Knorr hut sits at the western end of the foot of the Brunntalkopf (2 hrs from the Reintalanger hut).

b) From the Ehrwald alm branch left off the road just before you reach the stream and before it starts to climb steeply to the right. Go past the plague chapel, then climb in hairpins through a belt of trees onto the tongue that reaches down from the Gatterköpfe, and continue up to the Feldernjöchle gap (2024m), where the route is joined by two paths from the Leutasch valley. Now go left down a short steep slope, then equally steeply up again, and finally over the rock to the famous Zugspitzgatterl gap, which marks the frontier (2 hrs from Ehrwald alm). A pretty path goes gently up to the frontier guards' hut and then in a sweeping curve, more or less level, to the Knorr hut (1 hr from Zugspitzgatterl).

c) Those who like the easy life may take the cableway to Zugspitzkamm, walk through an interesting ice tunnel to the Schneeferner-Haus and stroll painlessly across a vast sandy scree run and down to the Knorr hut.

Summit ascent

From the Knorr hut walk 5 mins. up the Zugspitze path and then to the right on a waymarked path up to the foot of the rock spur. Climb a gully going to the right up onto grass and then go diagonally right again, across a scree gully up to the ridge on a level with the Brunntalkopf and a little above the lowest gap. Now follow the waymarks and the occasional wire ropes. The route is sometimes on the ridge, sometimes to the west, and its rich variety will amply reward your exertions as it leads you up to a gap not far below the summit. A few minutes uphill and eastwards takes you onto the Jubiläumsweg at a point on the Höllentalgrat east of the Innere Höllentalspitze. The short scramble westwards to the summit involves climbing down one vertical and exposed rock step, but it is well protected.

Descents
As ascents. If you chose ascent c) and are still feeling adventurous, you may like to renounce the cableway all the way down from the Zugspitzkamm and, instead, scramble down to the Wiener Neustadt hut by the climbing path (see Route 13), before returning from there to the car park by the lower station.

Difficulty
Including ascents to the Knorr hut, very strenuous. If you approach through the Partnachklamm, it is advisable to make a night stop at the Knorr hut or the Reintalanger hut. Going up by the cableway makes the tour much less strenuous, but on no account underestimate the descent via the Zugspitzgatterl to Ehrwald, or the return to the Schneeferner-Haus and the Zugspitzkamm. The climbing path to the summit, and the one from the Zugspitzkamm to the Wiener Neustadt hut if you opted for that route, require a good measure of surefootedness and freedom from vertigo.

Times
Partnachklamm - Knorr hut 7-8hrs; Ehrwald alm - Knorr hut 3hrs (or, walking all the way from Ehrwald, 6hrs); summit ascent 2½hrs.

Bases
Knorr hut (2051m); service end May - 1 Oct; 17B, 80M, 20L. Reintalanger hut (1366m); service end May - mid Oct; 31B, 34M. Schneeferner-Haus (2650m).

Altitude differences
Partnachklamm - Knorr hut c.830m; Ehrwald alm - Knorr hut 558m; Zugspitzkamm - Knorr hut 754m; Knorr hut - Innere Höllentalspitze 692m.

Climbing path altitude
c.650m.

16. MITTLERE HÖLLENTALSPITZE 2740m
JUBILÄUMSGRAT
Wetterstein, Blassenkamm ridge

The Blassenkamm ridge runs east from the Zugspitze, over the Hochblassen and the Hohe Gaif to the Mauerscharte gap, forming the watershed between the Höllental to the north and the Platt and the Reintal to the south.

The section of the ridge from the Zugspitze to the Signalgipfel peak of the Hochblassen is called the Höllentalgrat, and the famous Jubiläumsweg, a 6-9hrs ridge climbing route, goes right along the top of it,

Jubiläumsgrat from the east, with the Zugspitze in the background, the Höllental to the right.

over the three peaks of the Höllentalspitze (the Innere H., the Mittlere H. and the Äussere H.) and the Vollkarspitze, down to the so-called Falsche (false) Grieskarscharte gap, over the west wall of the Hochblassen-Signalgipfel and down to the actual Grieskarscharte.

The whole of the route is a favourite among the more expert of rock-climbers; but the eastern section - from the Innere Höllentalspitze to the Alpspitze - is at least adequately protected, and there are two reasonably easy ways onto the ridge: by the climbing path from the Knorr hut, or over the Alpspitze. As a result the complete sequence - ascent to the route, passage along the protected section of the ridge, and final descent - adds up to one of the finest experiences of the pleasures of the climbing-path to be had in the northern limestone Alps.

Approaches
As for Routes 10 and 15.

Ascents
Via Knorr hut (see Route 15); via Alpspitze or Grieskarscharte gap (see Route 10).

Ridge route
From the east summit of the Zugspitze a well worn path leads to the top of the climbing path down to the Höllental, which is where the unprotected part of the Jubiläumsgrat ridge begins. Follow the same path eastwards along, or just below, the edge of the ridge, partly over easy walking terrain but also along a few very exposed sections of ridge or terrace. Note that it is absolutely essential, when you reach the scramble down the final rock tower onto the gap before the Innere Höllentalspitze, and for the following traverse up the almost vertical slabs of the south face, where there are very few hand-holds, that all but the most experienced climbers move only with proper rope protection. The ordinary climbing path tourist must not attempt this section except in the company of a climber of sufficient experience to be able to lead and provide a secure belay from above. From the gap the route goes to the right, then left again, and then straight up until it reaches the first wire rope. Simply follow the wire ropes up to the summit of the Innere Höllentalspitze (2737m. 2-3hrs). The worst, you will be relieved to know, is now over. From here to the Grieskarscharte gap all the difficult sections have wire rope protection. Continue along the ridge (past the sign where the protected path to the Knorr hut forks right), over the Mittlere Höllentalspitze (2740m), and on to the aluminium Höllentalgrat hut (1-2hrs), which was rebuilt in 1963 by the DAV Munich section to provide emergency accommodation. From the hut climb to the Äussere Höllentalspitze (2716m). If visibility is not good, be very careful to bear right beyond the summit, because it is easy to leave the route onto a side ridge which falls steeply into the Höllental. Follow the main ridge into a gap, then climb again up a steep and rather exposed section onto the Vollkarspitze. Now down and up again, until you reach the lower end of the wire ropes leading up the Hochblassen. Here follow the visible tracks left and down, but do not overshoot. Traverse along the bottom of the west face of the Signalgipfel summit of the Hochblassen. Follow the foot of the rock gently uphill onto the scree between the Hochblassen and the Grieskarscharte and scramble down the clear tracks into the gap (3-4hrs).

Descents
All descents lead down from the Grieskarscharte gap, so you must

make the turn down towards it, and not take the route onto the Hochblassen.

a) From the Grieskarscharte bear east into the Grieskar combe. From here the best route first makes a little climb onto the grassy saddle above the Bernardeinwände cliffs, then continues down to the Kreuzeckhaus hut by way of the *Schöne Gänge*. (See Route 10 (a))

b) From the Grieskarscharte head west to Hammersbach by way of the climbing path down into the Mathaisenkar. (See Route 10 descent)

c) From the Grieskarscharte go north up the climbing path to the summit of the Alpspitze, and from there down one of the three climbing paths to the Osterfelderkopf cableway, or to the Kreuzeckhaus hut. (See Route 10)

Difficulty
In good conditions, moderately difficult, but long, and extremely tiring because of the many counter-climbs. Dangerous in bad weather, especially snowstorms or thunderstorms.

Altitude differences
For ascents, see Routes 10 and 15, many counter-climbs on the ridge itself.

Climbing path length
c.3km

Times
Knorr hut - Höllentalgrat hut (bivouac) c.3hrs; Bivouac - Osterfelderkopf cableway or Kreuzeck c.6hrs; Bivouac - Grieskarscharte gap c.3hrs; for other times see Routes 10 and 15.

Bases
As for Routes 10 and 15; emergency accommodation in the Höllengrat hut bivouac for 6-8 people, open at all times, lightning-proof.
See sketch map p.61.

17. HOCHBLASSEN 2706m
Wetterstein, Blassenkamm ridge

The double summit of the Hochblassen is one of the mightiest of the many natural fortresses in the Wetterstein. Seen from the surrounding valleys it looks unremarkable. But from the Alpspitze or from the Schachen, its massive rock formations cannot fail to impress. And the north face is even more spectacular: smooth and sheer, it boasts the most severe rock climbs of the Wetterstein group.

For the climbing path walker, all the easier ascents lead up the west

The route up the Hochblassen goes from the gap on the right by way of the gully in the centre, then up the arête on the right to the summit.

ridge, where the more difficult sections are protected with wire ropes.

If you are both experienced and blessed with more than ordinary stamina, you could consider combining the asent of the Hochblassen with a climb up the Alpspitze or the traverse of the Jubiläumsgrat ridge (see Route 16).

Approach
As for Route 10.

Ascent
Access is from the north, so you will first have to get to the Grieskarscharte gap. The quickest way is from the Kreuzeck and up the *Schöne Gänge* (see Route 10).

When you reach the grassy saddle at the upper exit of the *Schöne Gänge*, continue over more grass southwards; then, keeping as close as you can to the corner buttress of the Alpspitze, reach the scree above the Stuibensee. Now, keeping a little below the rock spurs, climb gently into the Grieskar combe.

The path continues over snowfields, then climbs through the crags to the Grieskarscharte gap (c.2¾hrs), where the Jubiläumsweg climbing path ends (see Route 16). From the gap turn south onto a scree on the east flank of the ridge connecting the Alpspitze with the Hochblassen, just below the edge. Cross the scree and make for the point where the connecting ridge meets the rock face of the Hochblassen. Just below this point is a tiny gap, through which you can get onto the west flank of the ridge by scrambling down a short protected gully, almost as tight as a chimney. Now traverse round the west side of the rock face to where the route turns to climb, over scree covered rock, straight up onto the top of the ridge between the Vollkarspitze and the Hochblassen (½hr from the Grieskarscharte). The track divides here at a waymark on the rock which will point your way onto the Hochblassen.

Beyond the ridge, scramble down a gully about 3m long, then immediately bear left (eastwards) up into a small gap and down again for a few metres. (Try to make a mental note at this point for your return journey. Remember that, once back at the end of the wire ropes, you will need to turn westwards and scramble back up to the top of the ridge.) But for now, continue parallel with the top of the ridge until you reach a gully, full of slabs, and scale it with the help of some wire ropes. Pass behind a rock flake on the left onto a rock bastion, and traverse across large slabs to where the ridge meets the wall of the Signalgipfel summit. Now bear left and squeeze between another rock flake and the face, to reach a large, scree filled depression. Wire ropes will lead you up a broad chimney to a gap in the west ridge of the Signalgipfel at a point where a steep snow couloir falls to the north. From the gap, keep just to the Grieskar side of the ridge, then scramble up another chimney to a second gap, and from there straight up to the Signalgipfel summit (2698m; ¾hr from the Vollkarspitze-Hochblassen ridge). From the top, follow the ridge down again, alternating between the edge and the Reintal side, to the lowest gap, and finish with an easy stroll to the main summit.

Descent
Ascent in reverse as far as the Grieskarscharte and the end of the Jubiläumsweg. Be very careful when you reach the large, scree filled depression mentioned above. On no account bear right to start down the Höllental (north) side. You must first cross over onto the Reintal (south) side of the ridge to the wire ropes, which then lead you down safely. From the Grieskarscharte you have a choice of descents or continuations:
a) As ascent: to the Kreuzeck by way of the *Schöne Gänge*.
b) Down into the Mathaisenkar combe (see Route 10).
c) Up the south ridge of the Alpspitze. For descent, see Route 10.
d) Up to the Höllentalgrat hut (bivouac) by the Jubiläumsweg climbing path (second part of Route 16 in reverse), and descent to the Knorr hut.

Difficulty
Includes some quite testing rock sections; sparse protection, parts of which are in bad condition.

Altitude differences
Garmisch - Hochblassen c.1980m; Kreuzeck - Hochblassen 1057m.

Climbing path altitude
c.80m

Times
Kreuzeck - Schöne Gänge - Hochblassen 4½-5hrs; Grieskarscharte - Hochblassen 1¾hrs.

Bases
See Routes 10, 12 and 15.
See sketch map p.61.

KLETTERSTEIG

18. PARTENKIRCHENER DREITORSPITZE, WEST SUMMIT 2633m
Wetterstein group, Wetterstein ridge.

The Partenkirchener Dreitorspitze is one of the most striking rock masses in the southernmost of the three Wetterstein ridges, which is also the most formidable of the three. This excursion is highly recommended, even though the ascents to the summit are long and tiring and the fine rock section is only short. Over the years after the Hermann-von-Barth-Weg had fallen into disuse, the protection had badly deteriorated, but more recently the whole climbing path has been completely repaired by the Garmisch section of the DAV. And with good stamina and a slightly higher degree of skills, you can even add the summit of the Leutascher Dreitorspitze to your collection on the same outing.

Approaches
You can climb to the Meiler hut from the Leutasch valley, or from Garmisch-Partenkirchen, or from Klais. The approaches from the Leutasch side are much quicker as they start from 1100m, whereas those from Garmisch start from only 700m.
a) From the north, take the B11 to Mittenwald and turn off the by-pass through the town centre. The road up the Leutasch valley goes off to the right just before the end of the town. Continue up the valley to the western edge of Lochlehn, where the ascent up the Berglental valley begins.
b) From Garmisch via the Partnachklamm.
c) From Klais (railway station) on the B2 Garmisch-Mittenwald road.

Ascents to the Meiler hut
a) Up the Berglental valley. 100m. west of the last house (No.231) in Ober-Lochlehn, at the edge of a wood, is a gate and a signboard pointing into the trees. Follow the sign half-left to a tree (by a wooden seat) painted with a prominent waymark. Now follow a distinct track and the red - *not* the blue - waymarks, first across another, rather clearer, track, then to a stream. From the west bank a waymarked footpath will take you in 10 mins onto another track, again with red waymarks, and in another 10-15 mins. to the junction with the path to the Meiller hut from Puitbach and Oberleutasch. From here on the route is waymarked and clear, with no further forks or turnings.

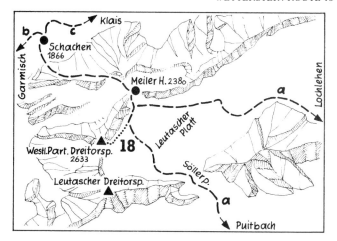

(Alternatively you can reach this junction from Puitbach by walking 650m up the track next to the Pension Dreitorspitze (no motor vehicles) as far as the edge of the trees, and then following the waymarks for c.30 mins.)

The route continues up the west side of the deep Berglenklamm gorge, threads its way through Latschen around the eastern slopes of the Äfelekopf, and then climbs steeply up the Berglenboden. There the path crosses to the other side of the valley, below the south face of the Musterstein, and finally climbs to the hut in steep zag-zags over loose rock and scree.

b) From Garmisch through the famous Partnachklamm gorge. Beyond the gorge, where the path divides, you have a choice of two routes to the Schachen. Either continue straight up the valley, finally turning left up the Oberreintal, or branch left to go via the Wetterstein alm and along part of the Königsweg. From the Schachen the Meiler hut is in sight in the gap between the Schachenplatte and the Frauenalpkopf. The path has in some places, been blasted out of the rock and is excellent.

c) The easiest route to the Schachen is from Klais. Take the metalled toll road to Schloss Elmau (1½hrs. on foot). By the inn in the village of Elmau turn into a good dirt road (called the Königsweg), which climbs gently up to the Schachen via the Wetterstein alm.

The Dreitorspitzen from the Gaifkopf.

WETTERSTEIN ROUTE 18

Summit ascent

From the Meiler hut take the old Hermann-von-Barth-Weg. It is rather decayed, but perfectly walkable, and the protection was all renewed some years ago. It first leads down to the edge of the sheer slabs of the Bayerläander Turm, traverses the rock near the bottom on wire ropes (memorial tablet) and continues down into the Leutascher Platt combe. Now climb again, first over fallen rock, then in two wide hairpins up the scree run below the rock face. The route makes for a barely protruding rock spur which projects from the buttress more or less directly in vertical line with the summit. Here, by a large boulder marked with paint spots (¾hr. from the Meiler hut), is where the actual climbing path begins. First climb almost vertically up some steel rungs, and take great care, because some of them may be loose. The route next levels out somewhat, follow wire ropes across crags and some gullies between rock slabs. About 80m below the ridge the track bears left and rises rather indistinctly over scree-covered crags onto the ridge at a point a little below the west summit and between the Partenkirchener - and the Leutascher Dreitorspitze. Now continue in a few zig-zags up the eastern, right-hand slope to reach the summit.

Descents

As ascents a) to c). For experienced rock climbers who decide to take on the Leutascher Dreitorspitze by crossing the connecting ridge (Grade II+), the best descent (which will require surefootedness and freedom from vertigo) is via the Söller Pass.

Difficulty

As a one-day tour, very arduous. From the Meiler hut (after overnight stop), an easy day. Freedom from vertigo and surefootedness required for the climbing path to the summit and, for those who opt for the extra climb, for the Söller Pass. In mist, route-finding is difficult on the Leutascher Platt.

Times

Leutasch - Meiler hut via Berglental valley 4½-5hrs; Partnachklamm - Schachen 5-5½hrs; Klais - Elmau 1½hrs; Elmau - Schachen 3½-4hrs; Schachen - Meiler hut 1½hrs; Meiler hut - west summit of Dreitorspitze 2hrs.

Bases

Meiler hut (2380m); service Whitsum - 1st week Oct; 18B, 70M, 20L. Winter shelter with 8M. Schachenhaus (hut) (1866m); summer service; 22B, 12M.

Altitude differences

Leutasch - west summit 1570 m; Garmisch - west summit 1930m; Klais - west summit 1680m; Meiler hut - west summit 253m.

KLETTERSTEIG

Climbing path altitude
c.150m.

Note
On the Schachen you can visit the Königshaus - a hunting lodge built in 1870 by Ludwig II of Bavaria - with its famous moorish room on the first floor (guided tour recommended). Near the house there is a very attractive alpine garden. Also nearby is the Schachenpavilion - a summerhouse standing on a rock platform over a sheer drop into the Reintal - which commands a memorable panoramic view of the massive, bare, rock horseshoe of the whole Wetterstein group.

19. HOHE MUNDE 2659m   NIEDERE MUNDE
Mieminger range

The bastion at the eastern corner of the Mieminger range is called the Hohe Munde. Its profile is handsome and unmistakable from every point of the compass, but it looks particularly impressive from the south, where it rises a clear 2000m above the floor of the Inn valley. The views from the summit are exceptional. Walkers and scramblers flock to its slopes in the late summer, while the south-east ridge and the south-west buttress seem irrestible to rock climbers in search of the extreme. The normal route to the summit is quite straightforward, but you will need some stamina and reasonable weather, for conditions can be pretty unpleasant on the ridges at 2600m in mist or snow.

Few people know of the climbing path from the summit across the rock on the south side of the ridge to the neighbouring Niedere Munde, and even fewer frequent it. Those who do are rewarded with a real surprise. From the normal route the Hohe Munde looks like a fairly ordinary mountain, but on this side it reveals rock scenery that is almost on a par with the Dolomites. The only pity is that the climbing path, with its wire ropes, is so short.

If you are not afraid of long approaches and even longer return routes, then you will certainly enjoy yourself on these lonely, airy rocks.

Approaches
From Obern (1166m) or Buchen (1210m), both on the edge of Leutasch.

Ascent to the Rauth hut
a)   From Oberleutasch continue south across the meadows of the

Weiler Obern towards the Weiler Moos. When the fence to your right ends, bear right on a path through the woods to a fork. Take care to follow the waymarks as you climb, first along a cart track and finally up a steep wood to the hut. (1½hrs)
b) From the lower station of the new chair lift, either ride up or walk to the hut up the wide path alongside the ski piste. (1½hrs)

Summit ascent
From the Rauth hut the route climbs, first gently, then more steeply across a grassy depression to the upper edge of what used to be the Moosalm meadows, at a point called the Jöchl - a very popular spot on account of the splendid views. Now take a steep path left through the Latschen and onto the broad, open slopes of the east summit. Here the path becomes clearer as it climbs in a series of steep and tiring zig-zags to the boulders of the east summit itself (2592m, also known as the Signalgipfel), where a whole array of aerials seem to be competing for pride of place with the summit cross.

From the summit plateau the path heads down - rather indistinctly - over scree and some rock steps to the Steinernes Mannl, a rock in the gap between the two summits. Now climb again - quite steeply in places - up the sometimes rather narrow ridge to the main summit (20-30mins). Your efforts will be rewarded with a view which is even more spectacular than that from the east summit.

Follow the ridge down towards the north-west, to where you can see a wire rope disappear down the south-west face. Scramble down the protections to an easy rock couloir, taking it slowly enough to enjoy the astonishing natural sculpture of the rocks. The next section used to be a Grade I rock climb among slippery ledges and rock gullies, but today the traverse across the shattered cliffs of the Obere Fürleg and the Zintergrat ridge to the top of the Niedere Munde - the mountain's western bastion - is easily negotiated along excellent wire ropes. Before the present protection had been installed, however, this splendid peak was accessible only to the few scramblers who had the skill and confidence to tackle the Grade II climbs along the jagged ridge between the Hohe Munde and the Niedere Munde.

Descents
a) Walk down the broad flank of the ridge to the saddle (Niedermundesattel, 2055m). Now turn north and zig-zag down the waymarked path (No.811) through a wide belt of Latschen to join a road (no motor vehicles allowed) near the Tillfussalm (1393m) and the Gaistalalm (1356m). A very long walk down the road will

View to the north west from the summit of the Hohen Munde. In the background is the Zugspitze with the Jubiläumsgrat (right) and the Schneefernerkopf (left).

bring you back to your starting point.
b) From the Niedermundesattel take the steep path down the south side as far as the inn at the Strassberg, then walk through the Strassberger Klamm gorge in the direction of Telfs as far as Ebenat. The return journey to your starting point is by a very long and complicated slog along paths and little roads, by way of Birkenberg or Brandt. (A much better idea is to have a car parked at the Strassberg Inn.)

Difficulty
In good conditions, a simple excursion with no technical problems, but very long and tiring.

Altitude difference
1530m

Climbing path length
c.400m

Times
Valley floor - Rauth hut 1½hrs; Rauth hut - summit 2½-3hrs; either descent 3-5hrs.

Base
Rauth hut (1598m); service all year, overnight accommodation; beautifully sited on a plateau at the tree-line, with splendid views; accessible by chair-lift.

Note
Too long and tiring for children and the unfit!

20. EHRWALDER SONNENSPITZE 2417m
Mieminger Range

The Mieminger range stands like a mighty dividing wall between the valleys of the Inn and the Gaistal, running from the Buchner Sattel gap in the east to the Fern Pass in the west. Its most handsome summit is the Sonnenspitze, at the end of the longest of the northern subsidiary ridges of the range. It and the Hohe Munde share the top spot in the popularity stakes in the western parts of these mountains.

The climbing path I shall describe makes its ascent from the south. But it is not waymarked and protection has only been installed at the most difficult points. This, and the nature of the terrain, makes it, in terms of required technique, the most difficult tour in the book. It should be rated as a Grade II (Moderate) rock climb.

Approaches
a) Via Garmisch to Ehrwald (966m). At the church, turn right (eastwards) along a decent road going towards the Ehrwalder Alm. Continue through Oberdorf to the barrier at the lower station of the chair-lift.
b) From Biberwier (911m), the next village south of Ehrwald.

Ascents to the Coburg hut
a) Take the chair-lift (23mins) to the upper station by the Ehrwalder Alm. Go past the Alpenglühn Inn, then a little way along a road and over a stream. Now bear right up the wooded slope and slightly down again to the road from Leutasch and the Gaistal valley. Turn right along the road or, for a much pleasanter walk, branch left after c.500m, just before a forest track, onto a

KLETTERSTEIG

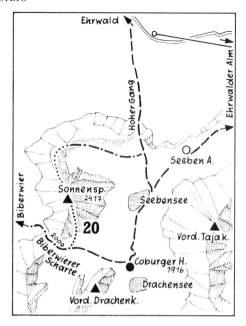

footpath. This will lead you almost level along the foot of the north side of the Vorderer Tajakopf to the Seebenalm, and after another 15mins to the delightful Seebensee. The path continues from the south end of the lake, climbing in a long series of zigzags through Latschen to the hut. Only residents are authorized to drive to the Ehrwalder Alm, but the proprietor interprets this to include overnight visitors to the inn.

b) Via the Hoher Gand (high passage). Turn right off the road at a little chapel just before the lower station of the chair-lift, cross the stream and take a footpath across some marshy meadows. Follow the waymarks up through the conifers towards the rock face of the Seebenmauer. Continue through Latschen and across a screerun to a prominent corner, where you can sit down and enjoy the view from a bench kindly put there by the Coburg section of the German Alpine Club. The next section begins through Latschen, but continues up to the Seeben plateau on wire ropes over rock, and demands a little sureness of foot and some measure of freedom from vertigo. From the plateau, walk gently down to the

lake and continue as in a) above.
c) Via the Biberwierer Scharte gap. Walk south from Biberwier past the Rochus chapel in the Lärch meadows at the foot of the Sonnenspitze, and up to the edge of the woods. A few metres to your right you will see a wide, gently rising track - once the access road to a now disused mine. Our path - clearly waymarked - is to the left of the track. It starts through the wood, then zig-zags up through Latschen and screes to the Biberwierer Scharte (1999m), which is the col between the Sonnenspitze and the Schartenkopf. From the col, either bear left for the summit ascent, or continue straight on for 15mins to the Coburg hut.

Summit ascent
To reach the south face ascent, take the path from the Coburg hut round the north of the Vorderer Drachenkopf, through the Schwarzkar combe, and on towards the Biberwierer Scharte gap until you reach a Latschen covered shoulder reaching southwards from the Sonnenspitze and far into the combe. Our route starts up an indistinct track through the scree to the east of the shoulder, then mounts the spur itself and climbs up some ribs and gullies to the bottom of the face of the crags. Now climb to the right and into a very steep and narrow couloir. Your next objective, which is to climb up and out of this couloir, will require some climbing skills. Once out of the top, scramble, with the aid of two blessedly solid iron rungs, round a small but awkwardly projecting boulder to reach a comfortable stance. The continuation to the left and onto the rock face used to be protected by a wire rope but, alas, it came away a few years ago. So now your way forward is to use an artificial hand-hold near the foot of the wall to edge your way out across the face, until you can get hold of the one remaining (and solid) wire rope to ease your passage along a horizontal ledge c.20m long. Be very careful to fix a clear picture in your mind's eye of the last iron anchorage, because this spot will be the vital key to your descent!

From the end of the ledge, head diagonally up to the bottom of a rather steep, wide gully. Climb up a series of fairly straightforward artificial steps to the cairn at the top and traverse right to a scree filled gully plunging down from the summit. Either climb the gully, or take the clearly visible track up the slightly less steep ridge to the right until the route levels off to reach the south summit (2412m). To reach the main summit, follow the ridge down for a few yards, then climb over some very exposed boulders to the gigantic summit cross, erected in 1974.

KLETTERSTEIG

The climbing pitch has recently been eased just a little by the local mountain rescue organization, who have fixed a number of bright red abseiling pitons. These will allow the less experienced and the timorous to be afforded proper rope protection by their braver and more adept companions.

Descents
a) As ascent. This is the recommended descent because its route is easiest to follow.
b) Down the north-east shoulder. When you reach the scree gully between the two summits, exit as soon as possible and make a long, slanting traverse below the summit cliffs to a rock rib. Now follow a visible track to the edge of the Latschen and down to the south end of the Seebensee. From here, the best way back to Ehrwald is by the Hoher Gang.
c) Down the steep north shoulder by way of a faint track - equipped with more red abseiling pitons - straight down to the Hoher Gang.

Difficulty
Average day excursion in length, but technically very demanding (Grade II). You will not only need to be experienced, perfectly footsure and absolutely free from vertigo, but will also require some climbing skill and be adept at route finding. Danger of rock falls from scramblers ahead. Do not attempt in misty conditions. Apart from the red abseiling pitons, the only visible points of reference are a few marker poles set among loose rocks. Children, and all but the most experienced scramblers, must be roped. On no account to be attempted by novices.

Altitude differences
Ehrwald - Ehrwalder Alm c.500m; Ehrwalder Alm - Coburg hut 416m; Coburg hut - Sonnenspitze 500m; Biberwier - Biberwierer Scharte 1008m.

Climbing path altitude
400m

Times
Chair-lift lower station - Ehrwalder Alm (on foot) 1¼hrs; Ehrwalder Alm - Coburg hut 2¼-2½hrs; chair-lift lower station - Hoher Gang - Coburg hut 2¾hrs; summit ascent 1½-2hrs; Biberwier - Coburg hut 3hrs.

Base
Coburg hut (1916m), German Alpine Club; service Whitsun - end September; 4B, 80M, 20L.

Note
If you are forced to give up and turn back, or if you finish the route with energy to spare, you could try one of the following substitutes/bonuses to be

found in these incomparably beautiful mountains:

Vorderer Drachenkopf (2301m) Waymarked route up the south-west ridge (Grade I). 1hr from Coburg hut.

Hinterer Tajakopf (2409m) Approach from Hinteres Tajatörl gap (Grade I). 1½hrs from Coburg hut.

Vorderer Tajakopf (2452m) Either from the Hinterer Tajakopf by an unmarked traverse of the west wall which can only be recommended to scramblers who are familiar with the area. Or by an equally unmarked route direct from the Coburg hut. (Both routes 2hrs and Grade I.) The most interesting descent is by way of the Hinteres Tajajöchl into the Brendlkar combe and down to the lovely, romantic Brendlsee. This excursion can be made to take in all four of the high altitude lakes in the Mieminger range, and a few more little tarns as well.

KLETTERSTEIG

From the Mittenwalder Höhenweg. In the middle distance - Erlspitzgruppe and the Freiungspitzen; in the background - Kalkkögel and Stubai Alps.

Karwendel

21. MITTENWALDER HÖHENWEG AND WESTERN KARWENDELSPITZE 2385m
Karwendel, northern Karwendel range

The Mittenwalder Höhenweg is a true ridge route. It is one of the newest climbing paths in the northern limestone alps and is certainly the most entertaining in the Karwendel group. 5½km long, it was equipped in 1972-3 by the alpine guides of Mittenwald. The protection is well judged and incorporates 1500m of wire rope and 60-70m of steel ladders.

Approach
From the Mittenwald by-pass (B11) follow the signs to the lower station of the Karwendelbahn cableway (913m).

Ascents to the Karwendelgrube
a) Take the cableway to the upper station (2244m), where the Mittenwalder Höhenweg begins. This is the easy way.
b) The super-fit may like to take the tiring but interesting Karwendelsteig route. It first climbs in zag-zags through the upper forest to the Mittenwald hut (1½hrs). A further 2hrs. including a few wire ropes, takes you through the depression called the Wanne (tub) depression and over rock to the Karwendelgrube combe. Be warned that the last wire rope section is on the north-facing slope. In early summer be prepared to encounter old snow, and in autumn, new snow and ice.

Ridge route
I strongly recommend you to take the short climb to the summit of the Western Karwendelspitze (2385m) before setting out along the ridge. It involves only an easy 30mins. scramble from the upper cableway station, with some wire ropes to help up the last few metres.

The Mittenwalder Höhenweg proper starts at the highest and most southerly point of the path round the Karwendelgrube. The first wire ropes begin just by the German-Austrian frontier stone and launch you straight into the lofty, rocky, alpine world through which the

KLETTERSTEIG

route will be making its way (by wire ropes and ladders in the most exposed sections) for the next 3hrs. or so.

It sticks more or less to the ridge all the way from the Karwendelgrube to the Brunnensteinspitze, swinging to and fro between the German and the Austrian sides. The views are spectacular: east to the rest of the Karwendel group; west to the Wetterstein group and two lakes, the Lautersee and the Ferchensee; and south to the shimmering, snow covered peaks of the distant Central Alps.

The route first climbs onto the Northern Linderspitze (2372m), then goes down steep grass to the Steinerner Zaun (stone fence) (¾hr). It crosses the Heinrich-Noe-Weg, climbs again onto the ridge and over the Southern Linderspitze, and continues down to the Gamsangerl (1hr), where there is an escape route in case of bad weather down to the Sulzklammanger (¾hr) and then by the Heinrich-Noe-Weg either to the Brunnenstein hut (1½hrs), or back to the Steinerner Zaun and the cableway station (¾hr). But in reasonable conditions there is no need to deny yourself the pleasures of the remainder of the ridge route as it continues over the Sulzleklammspitze (2323m) and the Kirchlespitze (2302m). From here the descent leads easily down to the Brunnensteinanger (2082m). But don't leave the ridge without making the short ascents to the Rotwandlspitze (2193m) and the Brunnensteinspitze (2179m), so as to have the opportunity of enjoying some well-earned rest and refreshment at the tiny, venerable Tirol hut.

Descent

From the Brunnensteinanger via the Brunnenstein hut (1hr) to the lower Sulzleklamm gorge. Then return to the lower cableway terminus, either by a delightful forest path called the Leitersteig (involving some gentle counter climbs), or across the meadows of the Hoffeld.

Variants
a) The Heinrich-Noe-Weg is an easier variant of the Mittenwalder Höhenweg. It, too, starts on the path round the Karwendelgrube, but from a point only about half-way up. It first bears east, down to the Steinerner Zaun, where it crosses the ridge. It continues down the west side, sometimes on wire ropes, to the Sulzleklammanger, then through the upper trees of the Sulzlewald and via the Upper Sulzleklamm gorge to the Brunnenstein hut. This is a fine route in its own right, which takes about 5hrs. from the upper cableway station to the hut and back to Mittenwald.
b) A good shorter tour can be made by taking the Heinrich-Noe-Weg from the upper cableway station to the Sulzleklammanger, then climbing up to the Gamsangerl and returning to the upper station of the cableway by the Mittenwalder Höhenweg (1 hr). (This round trip works equally well - and takes the same time - in either direction.)

Difficulty

If you use the cableway up to the start but walk back to the valley after the end of the tour, then this is a comfortable one-day excursion. But walking up as well as down will turn it into a very strenuous day, especially because you will then be on the ridge in the heat of the afternoon. Freedom from vertigo and surefootedness required for both Mittenwalder Höhenweg and Heinrich-Noe-Weg.

Times

Mittenwald - Karwendelgrube, via Mittenwald hut 3½-4½ hrs, via Dammkar hut 4-5 hrs (or 1-1½ hrs less for descent via either hut); ridge route

KLETTERSTEIG

Karwendelgrube - Brunnensteinanger 2½-3 hrs; Brunnensteinanger -Mittenwald 3-3½ hrs; Karwendelgrube - Heinrich-Noe-Weg - Mittenwald c.5 hrs.

Bases
Upper station of Karwendelbahn cableway (2244m); restaurant; no overnight facilities. Tirol hut (2100m); summer service; 6L. Brunnenstein hut (1560m); summer service; 30L. Mittenwald hut (1519m); service early May-Mid October, 40M.

Altitude differences
Mittenwald - Western Karwendelspitze c.1470m; the Mittenwalder Höhenweg fluctuates up and down around an average altitude of 2200-2300m.

Climbing path length
c.5½km.

Note
There is an interesting and rewarding route with some wire rope sections from the Mittenwald hut up to the Linderkopf.

22. FREIUNGEN-HÖHENWEG AND REITHER SPITZE 2373m
Karwendel, Erlspitze Group

This favourite high-level route has only a few wire rope sections, and so is really no more than a protected path. But the attractions of the landscape are so exceptional and the varieties of terrain so rich that I have no hesitation in recommending it to climbing path enthusiasts. If you can spare two days, then stop overnight at the Solsteinhaus (hut) and continue next day along the Gipfelstürmerweg to the Seegrube above Innsbruck. Add a third day, and you can crown a quite exceptional experience by completing the traverse of the whole Karwendel via the Goetheweg and the Wilde-Bande-Steig all the way to the Bettelwurf, by which time you will have spent three whole days at or around the 2000m line.

Approach
From the Seefeld by-pass (on the Scharnitz - Zirl road) follow the signs to the lower station of the Seefeld - Ross hut funicular (1234m; large car park).

For those not arriving by car, there is a good train service to Seefeld.

Ascent to the Nördlingen hut
The easiest way up to the Ross hut (1748m) is by the funicular, but the first train does not leave until 9.30. The walk up is rather tedious and

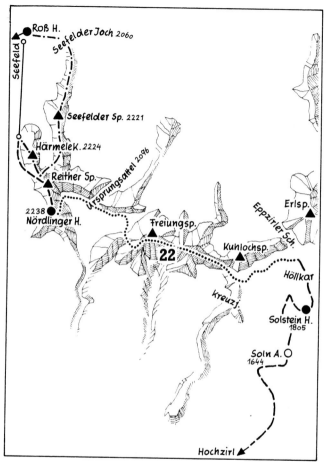

takes 1½-2 hrs. Disciples of the easy life will continue upwards by the cableway to the Härmelekopf (upper station, 2034m) and then choose between two path to the Nördlingen hut. The easier one, round the west and south flanks of the Reither Spitze, takes ½-¾ hr; the ridge route over the summits of the Härmelekopf (2224m) and the Reither Spitze 2374m takes ½ hr longer, plus an easy 10 mins from the second summit to the hut.

The Ursprungsattel with the Freiungspitzen (right) and the Erlspitze (centre). In the background the Kleiner Solstein and the Hohe Warte.

Freiungen Höhenweg ridge route

The route proper begins immediately behind the Nördlingen hut, which at 2238m is the highest in the Karwendel. It leads down steeply for c.20 mins to the Ursprungsattel gap (2096m), which is the lowest point on the route. Here a path branches north down the Eppzirl alm, but our route continues west across the grassy saddle, then round under the south side of the Wibertürme pinnacles, and now to the right, across scree, to the first wire ropes, which lead onto the south side of the Freiungspitzen. Soon after this the route reaches its highest point, continuing mostly on the south side but sometimes climbing onto the crest of the ridge. The views everywhere are memorable.

Parts of the route run along the foot of some magnificent rock, which may tempt summit-baggers to indulge in some little climbing detours onto the towers and pinnacles of the Freiungspitzen (2332m) and the Kuhljochspitze (2297m) - both Grade I. At the Kuhljochscharte gap (2171m) the Solsteinhaus first comes into sight, and the route leaves the south side of the ridge to turn steeply down to the north-east. (Watch out for the waymarks - No. 211 - and be careful not to take the unmarked path branching south, which leads to the Kreuzjöchl.) The next section is a rare visual treat. The route follows a bold line across the sombre, scree-filled Höllkar combe at the foot of the south face of the Erlspitze - a fantastic mosaic in which nature has splintered and shattered the rock into a myriad of weirdly-fashioned pinnacles and chimneys. If the whole route from the Nördlingen hut is a symphony of pleasures, then this last extraordinary scenery is a worthy coda.

Halfway across the scree the path divides. The waymarked path to the left (No. 212) climbs to the Eppzirler Scharte, but our route leads, rather indistinctly, down the scree and then, bearing left through Latchen, to the Solsteinhaus on the Erlsattel (1805m). If you have decided to stay overnight at the hut, and still have time and energy, then try the very rewarding scramble to the summit of the Erlspitze (2404m). The route is waymarked and protected; the view from the summit is magnificent. And just before you reach it, look down to your right for a glimpse of the astonishing Gipfelstürmernadel, a great blade of rock thrusting aggresssively up out of an ice-bound chimney. (Solsteinhaus - summit, 1½ hrs.)

The hut is the start of Route 23 (Gipfelstürmerweg), and of another highly-recommended route called the Zirler Schützensteig (Zirl Hunters' Path) to the Neue Magdeburg hut. (1½-2 hrs; good views; clearly waymarked; wire ropes and steel rungs; requires freedom from vertigo and surefootedness.)

KLETTERSTEIG

Descent

For the easiest way back to Seefeld, start westwards down the wild, romantic Erltal valley (waymarked No. 213), where some of the best sections will stir recent memories of the heights above. Pass the alm hut on the Solnalm (1643m) and continue down into the high Oberbach valley where, beside a cross and a spring, you meet the forest road coming up from Zirl. Follow it down to the first hairpin, where a signpost marked 'Hochzirl' points you down the old road to the idyllic little railway station of Hochzirl (922m). Take the (very cheap) train back to Seefeld and walk through the town back to the car park.

Difficulty

Even if you use the funicular up and the train back, you will find this a full day's walking. Requires surefootedness and moderate freedom from vertigo. In mist, be sure to watch out for waymarks. Take extra care if the path is wet.

Times

Funicular lower station - Ross hut (walking) 1½-2 hrs; Ross hut - Seefelder Joch (walking) ¾-1 hr; Ross hut - Nördlingen hut via Reither Spitze 1½-2 hrs; Seefelder Joch - Nördlingen hut via Seefelder Spitze and Reither Spitze 2-2½ hrs; Härmelekopf upper funicular station - Nördlingen hut ½-¾ hr, or via Reither Spitze 1-1½; ridge route Nördlingen hut - Solsteinhaus 4-4½ hrs (or 4½-5 hrs in the opposite direction); Solsteinhaus - Hochzirl railway station 2-2½ hrs.

Bases

Nördlingen hut (2238m); service Whitsun-Mid. Oct; 36B, 30M, 3L. Solsteinhaus (hut) (1805m); service Mid. May-Mid. Oct; 28B, 40M.

Altitude differences

Lower funicular station - Ross hut 516m; Ross hut - Reither Spitze 626m; Nördlingen hut - Solsteinhaus 433m (but lots of counter-climbing).

Ridge route length

5-6km.

23. GIPFELSTÜRMERWEG AND VORDERE BRANDJOCHSPITZE 2558m
Karwendel, Inn valley range

This high-altitude connection between the upper (Hafelekar) station of the cableway from Innsbruck onto the northern range and the Solsteinhaus hut, via the Frau Hitt, makes a fine day's outing. Even though not much of it could properly be called a climbing path, it makes an ideal link between the climbing path routes to the west

(Freiungen-Höhenweg to the Reither Spitze) and those to the east (Goetheweg and Wilde-Bande-Steig to the Bettelwurf), and as such it deserves a place on the Karwendel agenda of every climbing path enthusiast.

The route is equally pleasurable in the reverse direction, and so is the alternative from the Hafelekar onto the Brandjochspitze and back to the Seegrube.

Approaches
a) From Innsbruck.
b) From Zirl and the Zirler Berg, via the Mittenwald and Scharnitz to Innsbruck road.
c) From Seefeld in Tirol: see Route 22.

Ascents to the route
a) From Innsbruck drive, or take the funicular, to the Hungerburg (852m) and continue by the cable car (take the first run, at 8.00, if possible) up to the Seegrube (1966m) and straight on by the upper cableway to the very top station on the Hafelekar.
b) From Zirl to the Solsteinhaus. Turn off the main road by the Haus Zirler Berg (hotel), then take the metalled road under the new road bridge towards Hochzirl. After nearly 2km turn right onto a dirt road (even though it is, properly speaking, closed to all but local vehicles). Drive 400m, then fork right and drive a further 3.8km to a sign prohibiting all motor vehicles (including locals!). Find one of the few and rather cramped parking spots and continue on foot to the end of the road, just short of the goods cableway to Oberbach. Now zig-zag up through the dense woods, then past a shooting box, to the Solnalm (1643m). The path bears north into the wild, romantic Erltal valley, crosses the stream and climbs in two hairpins to the Solsteinhaus.
c) From Seefeld in Tirol take the funicular to the Ross hut (1748m), then the cableway to the Härmelekopf, and continue to the Solsteinhaus via the Freiungen-Höhenweg Route 22.

Ridge routes
From the upper cableway on the Hafelekar the path is clearly waymarked as it sets out towards the west, and it takes only about 15 mins. to transport you into totally alpine scenery. From the western end of the saddle it runs mainly along the south side of the ridge, passing below the summit rocks of the Seegrubenspitze (2350m) and the Kemacher (2350m). Neither summit has a proper path, but both

*The Frau Hitt is steeped in legend.
It is a popular objective for experienced scramblers.*

can be easily scaled in good weather, although a little care is required in early summer, when there will be steep snowfields to cross and the snow may be hard and icy. Once past these two peaks, the path dips to the Langer Sattel (long saddle) (2258m), where you need to take care not to miss the fork to the Frau Hitt. The path makes a longish descent along the bottom of the sheer south face of the Sattelspitzen, and then climbs a little to where the routes to the Brandjochspitzen and the Frau Hitt divide, just below the lowest gap in the ridge.

a) If your goal is the Brandjochspitze, then bear west for the Julius-Pock-Weg, waymarked and protected. It first climbs in a few zigzags up to the rock face and onto the sharp edge of the east ridge. The final section of the ridge alternates between the edge and the north flank. It would be awkward in parts, were it not for the wire ropes and a few artificial steps and holds that ease the way, but in snow and ice it can become quite difficult.

Descent: Go back to the junction and continue a little further towards the Langer Sattel to take either the easy path down to the Seegrube (1966m), or alternatively the longer path via the Höttinger alm and the Umbrügger alm all the way down to the Hungerburg.

b) If you are heading for the Solsteinhaus, you will do better to renounce the Brandjochspitze. Instead bear right at the junction and make for the Frau-Hitt-Sattel (saddle) (2234m), by the path along the western foot of the famous climbers' rock itself.

Now scramble down steel rungs and wire ropes over a rock step into the Frau-Hitt-Kar combe and down over broken rock to the little lake (1878m). At the lower end of the combe, where the path divides, bear left (the right-hand path leads down to Amtssäge sawmill) and down another rock step on wire ropes. Traverse above the Arzlerkar combe, through a scree gully at the foot of the ridge that runs down from the Hippenspitze, and then climb steeply up into the gap. Now there is another rise across rather trackless Latschen before you reach an indistinct and inadequately-waymarked path which leads down through meadows to the Wilde Iss combe (1450m) to meet the path from the Kirstenalm to the Solsteinhaus. The last section of the route runs westwards, dramatically overshadowed by the north faces of the Solstein, first following the stream and finally climbing up to the Solsteinhaus on the edge of the Erlsattel saddle.

Descents
As ascents a), b), or c), depending on whether you went from east to

KLETTERSTEIG

west or vice versa. Alternatively you can walk via the Kirkstenalm and the Gleierschtal valley to Scharnitz.

If you finish at Zirl or Seefeld and have to return to the Hungerburg, go by bus or train to Innsbruck, then take public transport No.1 to its Kettenbrücke terminus, cross the square and take the funicular back to Hungerburg.

Difficulty
Long and tiring in either direction but, if the weather is reasonable and there has been sufficient thaw, then you need fear no problems. In mist route-finding on the western section, especially from the Wilde Iss to the Frau-Hitt-Sattel, can be difficult. The eastern sections demand some freedom from vertigo: in snow they can be perilously slippery.

Times
Hafelekar - Frau-Hitt-Sattel 2-3 hrs; Frau-Hitt-Sattel - Solsteinhaus 3-4 hrs (but longer in reverse direction); Frau-Hitt-Sattel - Vorderge Brandjochspitze 1½ hrs.

Bases
Hafelekar upper cableway station (2256m); restaurant and bar; no overnight facilities. Berghotel Seegrube (upper cableway station) (1966); service all year; 30B. Solsteinhaus (hut) (1805m); service mid-May - mid-Oct; 28B, 40M.

Other possibilities: Höttinger alm (1473m); summer service; 20 straw beds: or Kirsten alm (1348m).

Altitude differences
Hafelekar - Solsteinhaus 463m (but many counter-climbs totalling c.1450m!); Frau-Hitt-Scharte gap - Vordere Brandjochspitze 324m; Hafelekar -Innsbruck 1695m.

Ridge route length
Hafelekar - Frau-Hitt-Sattel c.3km.

24. BIRKKARSPITZE 2749m, BRENDLSTEIG
Karwendel, main ridge

The Birkkarspitze is the highest peak in the Karwendel group. I recommend it to climbing path enthusiasts - even though the actual climbing path section to the summit rocks is very short - for the beauty of the landscape and the outstanding views, which reach all the way from the nearby alpine foothills to the Tauern and the Silvretta in the far distance. Do not struggle up the grindingly tiring Schlauchkar, but take the well-waymarked Brendlsteig. You will find it not only infinitely more pleasant, but also, surprisingly, less crowded. Moreover its course lies along a splendid ridge running over the three

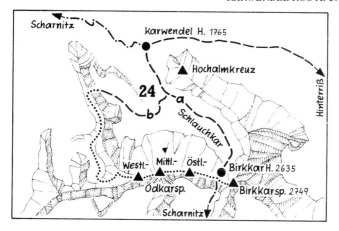

Ödkarspitzen.

Approaches
a) Take the B13 from Bad Tölz via Lengries and the Sylvenstein reservoir to the German-Austrian frontier, then turn onto the toll road to Hinterriss, which lies at the foot of the quickest ascent. If you want to save the second (Austrian) toll, leave your car in the car park in front of the Alpenhof (inn) (945) and walk a little way up the road to a signpost where a track turns right and up the Johannestal valley. (No motor vehicles).
b) A longer but even more beautiful way is via the second toll section of the same road to the Grosser Ahornboden (1218m). (See Route 26.)
c) Take the B11 through Mittenwald to Scharnitz (964), where tracks lead east into all the valleys that cut into the Karwendel on this side. (All closed to motor vehicles.)

Ascents to the Karwendelhaus hut
a) From the toll road walk for about 2 hrs up the Johannestal to the Kleiner Ahornboden, which must surely be one of the loveliest spots in the whole Karwendel. Here there are a few shooting boxes and, by the junction with the path to the Falkenhütte, a memorial to Hermann von Barth.

If you do not enjoy road walking, there is an alternative way to the Kleiner Ahornboden by a narrow, deserted forest path along the other side of the Johannestal. Leave the toll road just by the second toll station and walk across the meadows.

From the Kleiner Ahornboden the road starts south, next turns west in a sweeping curve, then climbs to the Hochalmsattel pass (1791m), and finally drops gently for the last few minutes walk to the Karwendelhaus.

b) From the Grosser Ahornboden take the pretty forest path to the Hohljoch pass (1795m) and across to the Falkenhütte hut (1846m), where there is a choice of routes. Either drop down to the Kleiner Ahornboden and continue as a) above, or avoid the loss of height by taking a shorter route along the foot of the cliffs of the Laliderwand to the junction with the road to the Karwendelhaus.

c) From Scharnitz turn left just before the church and follow the signposts to the beginning of the road up the Karwendeltal valley, passing the Larchetalm, the Angeralm and the Hochalm before winding its ways up to the Karwendelhaus (4½ hrs). Where the road begins to rise, between the Angeralm and the Hochalm, there is a possible short cut by forking right and climbing straight up to the hut. Be warned that this road to the Karwendelhaus is 18½ km long. Because most of it is fairly level, the best mode of transport is a bicycle. If you cannot carry bicycles in or on your car, you can hire them in Scharnitz.

Summit ascents

a) Follow the wire ropes up the steep slope next to the hut. Then traverse the Latschen on the west slope of the Hochalmkreuz and continue into the Schlauchkar combe, where the path divides, left to the Hochalmkreuz summit, right onto the Brendlsteig path. Go left, and up the combe over loose rock or old snow. At first the route is south-eastwards, then south up a steep and tiring section below the Schlauchkarkopf, and finally south-west up to the Schlauchkarsattel gap (2635m) and the tiny Birkkar hut (unlocked, unattended shelter). From the foot of the summit rocks, ¼ hr easy scrambling on wire ropes up the west ridge and finally over slabs and loose rock on the south-west side will take you up to the cross.

b) Follow route a) from the Karwendelhaus to the Schlauchkar for about 20 mins to where the paths divide, and take the right fork marked 'Brendlsteig'. After a gentle descent over grass, the path takes a sweeping curve round the combe to the foot of the steep

Latschen covered shoulder. A tiring scramble up wire ropes leads to the top of the ridge, where the route turns south to the foot of the rocks. The climbing path goes up the right-hand side, over some interesting sections, then leads over loose, shattered rock and stepped crags to the west ridge and the summit of the Western Ödkarspitze. From here follow the ridge over the Middle and Eastern Ödkarspitzen to the Birkkar hut; the wire rope protection is quite adequate and the views are spectacular. From the shelter, continue as route a) above.

Descents
As ascents a) or b). Or you can come down southwards on wire ropes down the Birkkar combe and into the Hinterautal valley. From there the walk back to Scharnitz leads through marvellous landscape with magnificent views of the north walls of the Gleiersch chain.

Difficulty
With an overnight stop at the Karwendelhaus, this is quite a tiring tour. With none, it is exhausting and very long. No technical difficulties, but in the upper part of the Schlauchkar there is grave danger of avalanches in the spring or after snow, and in autumn the old snow may be dangerously icy. On no account attempt to run down. In mist the route down through the combe may be difficult to find.

Times
Hintertiss - Karwendelhaus 3½ hrs (descent 2½ hrs); Grosser Ahornboden -Falkenhütte - Karwendelhaus 4-6 hrs; Scharnitz - Karwendelhaus 4½ hrs (descent 3½-4 hrs); Karwendelhaus - Birkkarspitze 3 hrs; descent from summit to Scharnitz via Hinterautal valley 5-6 hrs.

Bases
Karwendelhaus hut (1765m); service Whitsun - mid-Oct; 39B, 125M: passengers and/or baggage can travel from Scharnitz by jeep, Falkenhütte (1846m); service early June - early Oct; 34B, 69M, 20L. Hallerangerhaus hut (1768m); service Whitsun - early Oct; 20B, 60L.

Altitude differences
Hinterriss - Karwendelhaus 740m; Grosser Ahornboden - Karwendelhaus 575m (but considerable counter-climbs); Scharnitz - Karwendelhaus 800m; Karwendelhaus - Birkkarspitze 984m.

Climbing path altitude
114m.

KLETTERSTEIG

25. GROSSER BETTELWURF 2725m
Karwendel, Gleiersch - Halltal chain

The Bettelwurf is one of the highest and most imposing rock masses in the Karwendel. The summit is a formidable, broad pyramid towering almost 2000m over the Inn valley. And because it projects so far south, the views from the top are unparalleled.

The climbing path up the south side from the Eisengattergrat ridge is a relatively easy rock scramble, but it offers enough variety to be most entertaining.

Approaches
a) The simplest approach is from Solbad Hall to the Bettelwurf hut.
b) There is a good alternative approach from Innsbruck. Take the cableway to the upper station on the Hafelekar and continue along the so-called Innsbrucker Höhenweg. This is one of the finest ridge routes in the Karwendel, and goes via the Mandlscharte, the Goetheweg, the Pfeis hut and the Wilde-Bande-Steig climbing path to the Lafatscher Joch pass. (There is a bus back to Innsbruck from the end of the tour.)

Ascents to the Bettelwurf hut
a) Drive up the Halltal valley on the steep dirt-road (toll), past the inn at St.Magdalena and as far as the barrier at the Kronprinz-Ferdinands-Berg mine (4km from tollbooth). Walk on up the road, past several abandoned mine-drifts and the ruins of the artisan mine-owners' houses, then up to the Issjöchl pass and down to the Issanger. Now follow a wide, zig-zag path up the Latschen on the south slope to the broad dip of the Lafatscher Joch pass (2085m) and the crossroads with the path from the Pfeis hut to the Bettelwurf hut. Turn right and traverse the southern side of the Speckkar combe, more or less level, to the hut.
b) This is a shorter version of ascent a) (which I recommend for the descent). Called the Hirschbadsteig, it leads from the barrier by the car park, over the stream and through woods and meadows up to the Issanger.
c) The upper station of the Innsbruck cableway, at the Hafelekar, is connected to the Gleierschjöchl pass by the Goetheweg - a gentle, well-graded, waymarked and more or less level path with wonderful views (1 hr). A further hour will take you via two more gaps - the Mühlkarscharte and the Mandlscharte - to the Pfeis

KARWENDEL ROUTE 25

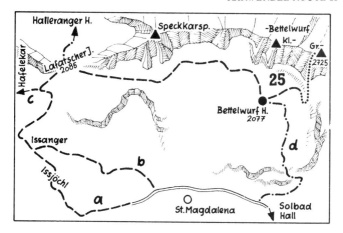

hut. Beyond the hut the route continues to the Stempeljoch pass (2215m) and then, by the wire ropes and steel rungs of the Wilde-Bande-Steig climbing path, to the Lafatscher Joch (2085m), where it meets ascent a) from the Hall valley. The continuous route from the Hafelekar to the Bettelwurf is generally known as the Innsbrucker Höhenweg and is famous for its magnificent and constantly-changing panoramic views. It runs almost level for its entire length and scarcely dips below the 2000m line. It is in itself a fine mountain tour, requiring only freedom from vertigo, surefootedness, and 4-5 hrs of time.

Summit ascent

From the hut follow the path east into a gully. Now climb steeply southwards onto the ridge, then north towards the foot of the rock, and from there up the Eisengattergrat ridge. The climb up to the summit ridge, mostly up adequate wire ropes to the right of a diagonal crack, is an exciting piece of climbing path. From the exit at the top, the summit is just a few metres to the east.

Descents

As ascents, or from the Lafatscher Joch by an alternative route via the Hallerangerhaus hut. From the pass this route goes north into the depression, past a spring and a tarn on the left, then down and to the right until it reaches a scree (the Lafatscher Durchschlag quarry). Next it runs along the foot of the great limestone slabs of the

Schnittlwände, then zig-zags down a scree gully and turns right, through magnificent pines to reach the Hallerangerhaus (1768m). The walk down the valley from the hut to Scharnitz is a pure joy.

Difficulty
If you have driven to the top of the Halltal valley, you might pack this excursion into one day, albeit a very long one. But by any of the other routes, an overnight stop is advisable. The Eisengattergrat and the Innsbrucker Höhenweg both require freedom from vertigo and surefootedness.

Times
Hall - Bettelwurf hut via Lafatscher Joch (driving as far as the barrier in the Hall valley) 2-3 hrs; Hafelekar - Bettelwurf hut 4-5 hrs; Bettelwurf hut -summit 2 hrs.

Bases
Bettelwurf hut (2077m); service mid-June - mid-Oct; 7B, 40M, 14L.
Hallerangerhaus (1768m); service Whitsun - early Oct; 20B, 60L.
Pfeis hut (1920m); service mid-June - mid-Oct; 30B, 47L.

Altitude differences
Hall - Bettelwurf hut c.1500m (or from car park by the Halltal barrier to Bettelwurf hut c.700m); Bettelwurf hut - summit 648m.

Summit climbing path altitude
c.500m.

Note
If you use route a), go and look at the chapel of St.Magdalena (1345m), which dates from 1486. It stands by the inn, and you can get the key from the landlord.

26. LAMSENSPITZE 2501m AND HOCHNISSL 2546m
Karwendel, Hinterautal - Vomper chain

The ascents of the Lamsenspitze and the Hochnissl are very popular mountain tours, and both hold some worthwhile pleasures for climbing path enthusiasts. With a bit of stamina it is not too hard to take on both peaks in one day, especially before or after an overnight stop in the Lamsenjoch hut. The few awkward sections on both climbs are well protected with wire ropes. And for experienced scramblers who are blessed with freedom from vertigo, the quickest and most exciting approach is a real treat: by way of an exposed climbing path - a real 'via ferrata' - up the almost vertical north precipice of the ridge joining the Lamsenspitze to the Hochnissl and then through the impressive natural Lamsentunnel.

KARWENDEL ROUTE 26

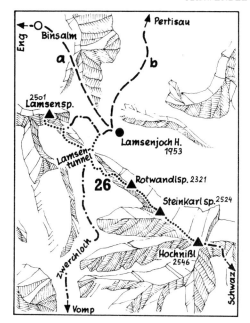

Approaches
a) From the north, drive by the B13 from Bad Tölz via Lenggries and the Sylvenstein reservoir to the Austrian frontier, then up the toll road through Vorderriss and Hinterriss to that most lovely of valley heads in the eastern alps, the Grosser Ahornboden (1218m). The shortest route up to the Lamsenjoch hut starts here, near the alm huts and the hotel 'In der Eng' which, although new, has lots of atmosphere.
b) Another good starting point is Pertisau on the Achensee and the prettiest way to get there from the north is as a) above to the Sylvenstein reservoir, but then left onto the road over the dam, along a section of the south shore, onto the so-called Deutsche Alpenstrasse to the Achen Pass, and down to the southern end of the Achensee for the turning to Pertisau.

Ascents to the Lamsenjoch hut
a) Leave your car at the car park of the hotel 'In der Eng', beyond which the road is closed to motor vehicles. So continue on foot to

105

The connecting ridge between the Hochnissl and the Lamsenspitze, showing its smooth east wall.

the little alm community in the middle of the valley floor, then turn left onto a narrow dirt road and follow it up to the Binsalm. (As this road is rather boring, you may prefer to go by the very steep, but shorter, old route from behind the hotel; it almost immediately crosses the stream - the Rissbach - and then climbs directly up to the Binsalm.)

From here the route continues steadily uphill through Latschen and alm meadows to the Western Lamsenjoch pass (1933m), before levelling out along a splendid high-level path to the Eastern Lamsenjoch pass and the Lamsenjoch hut, both already visible in the distance.

b) From Pertisau take the toll road up the Falzthurntal valley to the Grammai alm (1262m) and walk straight on and up many zig-zags to the hut (2 hrs).

Ascent to the Lamsentunnel

From the hut take the clearly-visible path west across the scree and boulders to the foot of the dark, uninviting north-east face. From this point on, be constantly alert to the danger of rock-falls. The wire ropes begin by a memorial tablet and are then continuous as the route gets progressively more exposed - indeed in a few places very draughty indeed - until they end at the dark entrance to the chilly Lamsentunnel. Hold onto the rope handrail to guide yourself through the first few yards of the dark tunnel, over muddy, slippery stones, then climb the steel rungs which ease the ascent up a vertical chimney and out into the daylight again on the far, south-west, side of the ridge. (There is a possible escape route from this point straight down to Vomp in the Inn Valley, via the Zwerchloch combe.)

Ascent from the Lamsentunnel to the Lamsenspitze

When you emerge from the tunnel take the right-hand path, which rises easily up to the Lamsenkar. Head for the north-west corner of the depression and the foot of two gullies which climb side-by-side to a wide scree-covered ledge between the Mitterspitze and the Lamsenspitze. The eastern one, called the Turnerrinne, used to be the favoured route, in spite of the frequent rock falls that rattle down it. But now there is a new, protected route, complete with wire ropes and some artificial steps, which climbs to the right of the gully and up to the crags below the scree-filled upper combe. Once in the combe, follow some very distinct tracks up the scree and loose rock towards the sheer faces of the summit ridge. Finally, a little below the top of the ridge, turn east and scramble to the summit up the scree on the south side.

Descent
Return to the Lamsenjoch hut, either as you came up, or from the upper combe back to the hut via the Lamsenscharte gap (2270m). This route, like the other, is protected with wire ropes, but it is rather less exposed and much shorter, so less experienced scramblers, or anyone with vertigo problems, may find it preferable in both directions.

Ascent from the Lamsentunnel to the Hochnissl
At the exit from the Lamsentunnel take the waymarked route starting slightly downhill to the right (east). It soon climbs again, fairly steeply, keeping a little below the top of the ridge, and finally zigzags up to the summit of the Rotwandlspitze (2321m). From here the route follows the ridge, first into a dip and then up again to the base of the summit rocks of the Steinkarlspitze (2524m). For collectors, the summit can be bagged by a short, easy detour. Then scramble by the wire ropes down into a gap by way of a chimney, finally climbing up again for the summit of the Hochnissl and a stupendous view into the Inn valley.

Descent
As ascent, or you can take the easy, but very long, route from the Hochnissl straight down to Schwaz.

Difficulty
Without an overnight stop the two summits in succession would make a very arduous undertaking. A night spent at the Lamsenjoch hut would make the Lamsenspitze a half day and the Hochnissl a short, or alternatively a very leisurely, day-tour. Both require surefootedness and a measure of freedom from vertigo, particularly in the Lamsentunnel.

Times
Grosser Ahornboden - Lamsenjoch hut 2 hrs; Grammai alm - Lamsenjoch hut 2 hrs; Lamsenjoch hut - Lamsenspitze 1½ hrs; Lamsenjoch hut - Hochnissl 3-4 hrs; Hochnissl - Schwaz 4-5 hrs; descent from top of Lamsentunnel via Zwerchloch to Vomp 4-5 hrs.

Bases
Lamsenjoch hut (1953m); service early June - end Oct; 29B, 72M.

Altitude differences
Grosser Ahornboden - Lamsenjoch hut 735; Grammai alm - Lamsenjoch hut 691m; Lamsenjoch hut - Lamsenspitze 548m; Lamsenjoch hut - Hochnissl 593m; Grosser Ahornboden - Lamsenspitze 1280m; Grosser Ahornboden -Hochnissl 1325m (plus counter-climb!).

Climbing path altitudes
Climbing path to the Lamsentunnel c.200m; climbing path alongside the Turnerrinne c.50m; climbing path sections of the Hochnissl summit ascent c.100m in total.

27. HUNDSKOPF 2243m AND WALDERKAMMSPITZE 2528m
Karwendel, Gleiersch - Halltal chain

To the east of the massive rocks of the Bettelwurf the ridge slopes away to end in a last and considerable summit called the Hundskopf. A modest climbing path was installed on its north face several years ago, which makes a rewarding half-day excursion.

Approach
From the motorway in the Inn valley (Solbad Hall exit) drive via Absam to Gnadenwald and, at the Hotel Speckbacher, take the metalled toll road to the Hinterhornalm (1522m; 6km from Gnadenwald).

Ascent
From the car park the path (red waymarks) crosses some meadows, climbs steeply through Latschen and then through easy crags onto the ridge. Now follow the ridge to where wire ropes lead up a steep, sharp rock edge. This is the old walkers' path. The new climbing path -called the Felix-Kuen-Weg - turns right just before this rock step, onto the north face of the mountain and to the first wire ropes. The route now traverses the whole width of the face, along natural rock ledges with plunging views into the Vomper Loch 1000m below, and soon reaches the saddle between the Hundskopf and the Walderkammspitze. Climb the steel rungs up an almost vertical rock step, and then scramble diagonally to the right up a gully (taking care at one large, loose boulder) to a platform. Continue up a steel ladder (c.5m) and some more steel rungs to the top of the summit ridge. The cross is just a few yards to the east, and commands splendid views in all directions.

The ladder on the Felix-Kuen-Weg.

Descent
a) The best way is down the east ridge, which is waymarked throughout and protected where necessary, back to the foot of the climbing path, and from there back to the Hinterhornalm by the ascent route.
b) Experienced scramblers may prefer to return to the saddle and then climb the very rewarding Walderkammspitze (2528m). From the saddle follow the unwaymarked but perfectly distinct track west, which goes all the way to the foot of the summit rocks, mostly along the top of the ridge, but sometimes just below along the south side. An easy, entertaining little climb from the north side (Grade I) will conquer the last few metres to the summit. (Not recommended in mist.)

Difficulty
The Hundskopf is an easy half-day excursion, but novices and children should be roped. Adding the Walderkammspitze makes the tour into an easy whole day, but is only recommended for somewhat more experienced scramblers.

Times
Hinterhornalm - Hundskopf 2 hrs; Hundskopf - Walderkammspitze 1 hr.

Base
Inn on the Hinterhornalm (1522m); 10B.

Altitude differences
Hinterhornalm - Hundskopf 721m; Hinterhornalm - Walderkammspitze 1006m.

Climbing path
c.300m.

The Sagzahn from the north.

Rofan

28. SAGZAHN 2239m
Rofan, main ridge

The delightful, easy high-level route from the Bayreuth hut over the Vorderes Sonnwendjoch, the Sagzahn, the Schafsteigsattel, the Markgatterl and along the side of the idyllic Ziereiner See includes a short, very simple climbing path up the west side of Sagzahn. Being only 50m high and protected with wire ropes throughout, it is ideal even for novices and children, provided ropes or self-belays are used.

Approaches

a) Via Kramsach (535m), in the Inn valley near Rattenberg. The most convenient approach is by the Rosenheim - Innsbruck

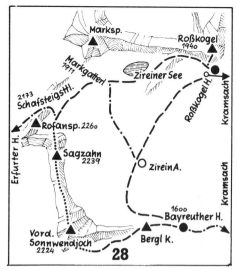

autobahn.
b) Via Murach (858m) on the Achensee, below the lower station of the Rofan cableway. The best approach is by the Achensee road, either through Tegernsee or via Bad Tölz and Lenggries.

Ascents to the Bayreuth hut or the Erfurt hut
a) If you are planning a one-day excursion, the Sonnwendjoch chair-lift will carry you conveniently up to c.1800m, and halve the time needed for the old walk to the Bayreuth hut through the Rotgschöss. From the upper station the path is clearly waymarked as it goes gently down over the Zireiner alm to the Bayreuth hut (1600m).
b) From Maurach, at the southern end of the Achensee, it is only a few minutes' ride by the Rofan cableway to the Erfurt hut (1834m). From the hut the path follows an interesting route via the Mauritz Hochleger, the Gruberstiege and the Gruberlacke tarn to the Schafsteigsattel gap (2173m) just below the main ridge (2 hrs).

High-level circular route and summit ascents
From the Bayreuth hut take the waymarked path round the Berglkopf, then zigzag up steep grass slopes and rock ledges to the

Sonnwendjochsattel (2134m). Walk up the grass hump to the ridge for a delightful view down to the Ziereiner alm. Continue left up the ridge and over some crags to the summit of the Vorderes Sonnwendjoch (2224m), with beautiful and extensive views (c.1½ hrs from the hut). A further ½ hr of easy and no less interesting path will take you onto the summit of the Sagzahn (2239m). This is where our climbing path begins. The protection is excellent as it plunges down the north-west face by way of a shallow chimney to the ridge below, where the route continues over grass to the Schafsteigsattel gap (2173m), to meet ascent route (b) above. From here the top of the Rofanspitze is only a simple 15 mins detour away. Head north-west, then swing round to the west over steep grass to the summit (2260m). From the summit follow the ridge east, almost back to the Schafsteigsattel, where the main route turns down between the Schokoladentafel (bar of chocolate!) and the east face of the Rofanspitze. There are some very exposed spots as it threads its way through crags and steep grass, along the tops of sheer drops, and down to the foot of the rock wall. The wire ropes on this whole section are in very poor repair, so great care is required especially in wet conditions.

From the foot of the rock wall the path heads down to the Markgatterl (1911m), first over loose rock, then through Latschen, all in the most romantic scenery and with wonderful views down onto the shimmering water of the Ziereiner See to the west and the Hirschlacke to the east. And if you look back at the precipitous cliffs behind, you will surely understand why rock climbers flock to the Rofan.

At the price of only 20 mins detour and 100m climb, an easy, mostly waymarked and always clearly discernible track will allow you to add the summit of the Markspitze (2011m) to your collection. And even for those who are unconcerned about summits, the magnificent views of the awesome northern cliffs of the whole Rofan ridge are more than sufficient reward for the little effort required.

Now return to the Markgatterl and walk east to where the path divides, right for the Bayreuth hut, left for the Rosskogel or the upper station of the chair-lift from Kramsach. If you are heading straight for the chair-lift, you have now only a pleasant stroll ahead: first 20 mins gently downhill through Latschen to the clear, tranquil water of the Ziereiner See, and then another 20-30 mins equally gently uphill to the station. But if you still have a little time, energy and will-power in hand, then you can close the full circle by a little detour onto the Rosskogel (1940m) before heading down to the chair-lift.

Descents

a) If you miss the last chair-lift, you can walk back to Kramsach down the ski-piste (2 hrs).
b) From the point after the Markgatterl where the path divides, you can walk to the Bayreuth hut (c.1 hr), and on through the Rotgschöss to Kramsach or Münster (a further 2 hrs to either village).
c) From the Schafsteigsattel or the Rofanspitze, go by ascent route b) to the Erfurt hut, and down to Maurach.
d) From the Markgatterl, you can reach the Erfurt hut via the Ampmoosboden and the Bettlersteig.

Difficulty

Day excursion. The climbing path on the Sagzahn and the descent beside the Schokoladentafel both require surefootedness and freedom from vertigo.

Times

Kramsach - Bayreuth hut 3 hrs (descent, 2 hrs); chair-lift upper station -Bayreuth hut 1-1½ hrs; Bayreuth hut - Sonnwendjoch - Sagzahn -Markgatterl - Ziereiner See - chair-lift upper station c.4-5 hrs; Erfurt hut -Schafsteigsattel 2 hrs; descent (on foot) c.4 hrs.

Bases

Bayreuth hut (1600m); service end May - Mid Oct; 23B, 34M. Erfurt hut (1834m); service Whitsun - October; 16B, 40M, 10L.

Altitude differences

Kramsach - Sagzahn 1704m; Maurach - Sagzahn 1381m; Bayreuth hut - Sagzahn, 405m..

Climbing path attitudes

Sagzahn c.50m; Schokoladentafel c.50m.

Note

Do not miss the remarkable Tirolean farmhouse museum near Kramsach, where 15 typical, authentic Tirolean farms dating from the sixteenth to the eighteenth century have been re-erected, to preserve for posterity (and especially for all true lovers of the Alps) some of the finest and most interesting examples of the Tirolean domestic architecture.

29. GUFFERT. 2196m.
Rofan

The Guffert is a bold, isolated pyramid of rock, falling away in a ridge to the east, with such fine views from the summit that it is a favourite outing for Munich mountain lovers. Climbing path enthusiasts whose ambitions are not too elevated will find the ascent up the north side an ideal last autumn outing - a chance to reflect and be tranquil.

The northern ascent is easy and the climbing path section is one of the shortest described in this book. Even beginners will find it within their powers if they are reasonably fit, and it can be combined with a descent down the south side to make an excellent day's outing.

Approach

Drive over the Achen pass via Tegernsee or Bad Tölz and Lenggries, then cross the frontier, and a few kilometres later turn onto a narrow winding road to Steinberg. Pass the sign marking the start of the path to the Guffert hut, and continue to the Unterberg alm (1004m), where there is space to park on the west side of the road, just before the bridge over the stream. Our route starts between the farm and the stream, up the wide dirt road. There is no signpost, but plenty of prohibition signs.

Ascent to the Iss alm

Start east up this road. After about 5 mins, at the first fork, branch left and continue northwards for about 30 mins until the road peters out. Here you should find a small red arrow carved into a tree and pointing straight up into the thick woods. There is no disernible path, but follow the direction of the arrow straight up the slope and in 15-25 mins you will strike the waymarked path from the Oberberg alm. If you do not like the idea of climbing with no path to guide you, then retrace your steps along the dirt road for a few minutes, to a barbed-wire fence enclosing a plantation of young trees. Now walk up along the fence until you reach the waymarked path just where the fence makes a right angled turn. From here the path rises gently through dense woods and curves round the west of the Guffert to the Stubach alm (1376m). Beyond the alm the route is well waymarked and offers some excellent views as it skirts the foot of the sheer north face of the Guffert - diving into and out of several deep gullies on the way - to reach the grassy shoulder well above the Iss alm visible below (1489m). Two other paths join our route at this point: one from the north, from the Ludwig Aschenbrenner hut via the Schneidjoch pass, and one from the east, from the Kaiserhaus hut. Continue south and head straight for the north face, where the beginning of the climbing path is marked with a red paint spot to the left of a small cave (15-20 mins from the shoulder).

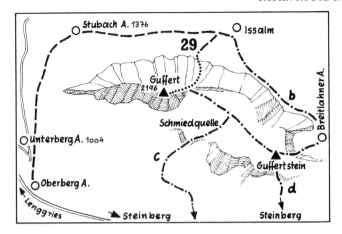

Summit ascent
At the entry a wire rope leads promisingly up over a 10-15m rock step and into a groove which climbs diagonally left until it widens into a depression. Now waymarks lead up onto a buttress projecting northwards, called the Tremelkopf, where there is a close-up view of the eastern part of the north face. Continue to follow the waymarks over grass and crags up to the summit ridge (1936m), where you meet the route from Steinberg. A further 15-20 mins easy scrambling along the ridge, over crags and broken rock and with the help of one or two wire ropes, will take you to the summit cross, where marvellous views will reward your exertions. Do not attempt the crossing to the west summit unless you are very experienced. It not only requires absolute freedom from vertigo, but also includes some Grade II pitches.

Descents
a) As ascent. Be very careful not to go all the way down into the gap on the green shoulder above the Iss alm to take the path westwards from there. The correct path is waymarked and leads down from a signboard about 100m before the bottom of the gap.
b) From the summit head down east, then up again to the saddle by the Guffertstein (1974m). Continue eastwards, down steep crags and green slopes, to the Breitlahn alm (1470M), then north-east along the foot of the north face to the Iss alm, and back to the Unterberg alm by the ascent route.
c) Go east from the summit, then bear right at the first fork, pass

On the most interesting section of the Guffert Northern ascent.

the famous Schmiedquelle spring and return to Steinberg by the popular southern path, first through Latschen, then in hairpins down through the mighty trees of the Bärenwald.

d) East from the summit to the Guffertstein, as for descent b), but then turn south. The path goes down through crags, grass and Latschen to a dry combe - the Luxeck-Waldboden (1727m) - then descends through woods to the Mühlegghof farm east of Steinberg.

Difficulty
An easy yet very rewarding day tour. The north ascent requires surefootedness, and the summit ridge, additionally, a measure of freedom from vertigo.

Starting points and times
Unterberg alm - Iss alm 2 hrs; Iss alm - Guffert 2 hrs; Steinberg - Guffert via Bärenwald 3½ hrs; Steinberg - Guffert via Luxeck 4½ hrs; Guffert hut - Iss alm 1¼ hrs.

Base
If required, Ludwig-Aschenbrenner hut - also called Guffert hut (1465m); service Whitsun - end Oct; 14B, 42L; winter shelter accessible with Alpine Club key, 4L.

Altitude differences
Unterberg alm - Guffert 1192m; Steinberg - Guffert 1181m.

Notes
I strongly advise against the ascent to the Unterberg alm from the signboard by the Zum Guffert-Aufsteig inn at the Obergberg alm (900m), because the waymarks have virtually disappeared.

If you have any time to spare at the end of the day, drive home via Achenkirch, where the little calvary with its 'holy steps' is a gem of vernacular devotional art.

On the Widauersteig. Shortly before the end of the long slabs, which lead to a gully between the Hackenköpfen and the Scheffauer.

Kaisergebirge

30. SCHEFFAUER 2113m
Wilder Kaiser

The Scheffauer stands at the western corner of the somewhat formless ridge which starts at the Sonneck and runs for about 3 km over the Zettenkaiser and the Zettenkaiserkopf before it drops into the Inn valley. The famous Widauersteig climbing path dates back to 1911. It is justly popular, for its wire ropes open up the varied pleasures of the north ascent even to relative novices, provided they are modestly free from vertigo. Using the chair-lift makes this a possible day excursion in the Wilder Kaiser from as far afield even as Munich.

Approach
From the Salzburg - Kufstein autobahn, take the Kufstein-Nord exit to the suburb of Sparchen and follow the signs to the lower station of the Wilder Kaiser chair-lift.

Ascents to the Kaindl hut
a) The quickest and most comfortable way is by the chair-lift. It climbs via the Brentenjoch gap in three stages and operates from 8.00. From the top station at Steinberg (1150m) it is only 20 mins walk to the Kaindl hut (1318m).
b) If you prefer to do more, but not too much more, of your own climbing up to the hut, take the alternative chair-lift, called the Kaiserlift, from just south of the lower station of the main lift, and ride up to the Berghaus Aschenbrenner inn (1140m). A pleasant, shady path - Jägersteig (hunter's path) - leads to the Brentenjoch (1204m), where you have a choice of routes to Steinberg. You can walk, mostly downhill, along the gentle path through the Gaistal valley, or alternatively ride up the third section of the Wilder Kaiser chair-lift. From Steinberg, continue to the Kaindl hut as on ascent a).

Summit ascent
From the Kaindl hut take the waymarked path south-east through

KLETTERSTEIG

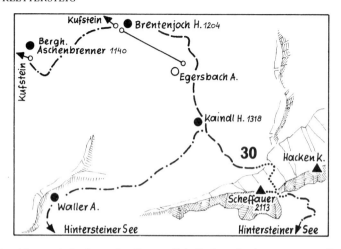

boulders and shrubs to the Grosser Friedhof combe (great graveyard). As you enter, bear left through Latschen onto the rib which encloses the combe to the east. The path traverses a scree-filled depression and then climbs steeply to the entry to the climbing path proper. Climb up a groove onto the slanting, stratified slabs that project from the rock wall. The route now goes right, along a ledge, to the deep gully between the Hackenköpfe and the Scheffauer, reaching the gully just above where it drops sheer. Follow the wire ropes up the gully, which contains one or two rock steps, through some crags, and up onto the gap. The summit is no more than 10 mins away to the west.

Descents

a) If you have to return to a car, scramble back to Steinberg as you came up, by way of the Kaindl hut. Now choose between walking or riding down by the chair lift. But if you want to go home with the happiest possible memories of your day, I suggest a compromise by taking only the first section of the lift, to the Brentenjoch, and walking from there. A few minutes' walk below the gap a sign bearing the legend 'Romantischer Weg nach Kufstein' (romantic path to Kufstein) points left to a path into the forest which will not only fully redeem its promise, but will even take you past a monument to Joseph Madersperger, inventor of the sewing machine! To return to Sparchen, take the Höfarter Weg from about 100m above Herr Madersperger. It

heads northwards, passes a monument to the economist Friedrich List, who died at Kufstein, and takes you back to the bottom station of the chair-lift in 20-30 mins.
b) If you are not tied to a car, go as far as the gap to the east of the summit and try the route south (waymarked, with some wire ropes) to Bärnstatt (924m) and the Hintersteiner See (883m) by way of the Steinerhochalm and the Hinterberg alm. Then either return to the Kaindlhut via the Walleralm, or walk down the so-called Steinerne Stiege (stone staircase) to the Steinerne Stiege inn (complete with bus stop) about 1 hr away at the side of the Kufstein - Ellmau - St.Johann road.

Difficulty
Easy day excursion if you use the lifts. The Widauersteig requires freedom from vertigo and surefootedness. Beware of rocks dislodged by other walkers higher up. Much more difficult in snow: take ice axes.

Times
Steinberg (top station of the Wilder Kaiser chair-lift) - Kaindl hut 20 mins; Kaindl hut - Scheffauer 2½-3 hrs; Bärnstatt - Schefauer 3-4 hrs.
Descents: Scheffauer - Bärnstatt 2½ hrs; Bärnstatt - Walleralm - Kaindl hut 2¼ hrs; Bärnstatt - Steinerne Stiege inn 1 hr.

Base
Kaindl hut (1318m); service all year; 15B, 30M.

Altitude differences
Kufstein - Scheffauer 1629m, Kaindl hut - Scheffauer 795m; Bärnstatt - Scheffauer 1195m.

Climbing path altitude
c.400m.

Note
Try to leave time to visit the castle at Kufstein. A useful guide *(Kleiner Urlaubsberater Kufstein)* is on sale at the ticket offices of the chair-lifts.

31. ELLMAUER HALT 2344m
Wilder Kaiser

The Ellmauer Halt - the highest peak in the Kaiser massif - is the summit of a gigantic, rather formless rock mass. Its awesome north face consists of sheer vertical slabs which rise 1150m straight out of the floor of the Kaisertal valley. Because of its central position, the summit commands impressive views.

The climbing path from the south side to the top via the Gamsänger is full of scenic interest and surely the most audacious in the Kaiser group. The course it follows makes the climb relatively simple, but there is ever-present danger of rock-falls.

Approach
From Ellmau (812m), on the Kufstein - St.Johann in Tirol road. At the eastern end of the village, turn right onto a narrow road to Wochenbrunn. Almost immediately, at a signpost, bear right again. Drive 3km to a large restaurant - the Gastwairtschaft Wochenbrunn - and then, on a toll road, another 1km to the Wochenbrunn alm, where there is a climbers' hostel and a large car park.

Ascent to the Grutten hut
The rather dull path begins as a mule track, then climbs steeply through Latschen to the Grutten plateau and the Grutten hut (1620m) 1¼ hrs).

Summit Ascent
Take the waymarked path from behind the hut up to the Hochgrubach combe at the foot of the towering 350m south face. Cross the screes below the Köpfeln and head for the grassy ledges -called the Gamsänger - that break the vertical precipices of the Kopftörlgrat ridge. Great care is required on these terraces because, although they are not all that exposed, they are frequently in the path of falling rocks. From the foot the wire ropes rise left, then negotiate a more craggy section and, at about 2120m, reach the yellow slab called the Jägerwand. The path which joins here is the old route from Hinterbärenbad, but it is presently impassible. Our route now climbs a wide groove towards a needle standing prominently on the ridge which rises to the Rote-Rinn-Scharte gap. Once on the ridge, continue upwards to a deep, dark, and very wet, cleft called the Achselrinne. The climb up the chimney is simple, thanks to steel pegs and a long, vertical ladder. Alternatively, you can scramble to the right of the cleft, up a narrow groove (good wire ropes) in a rock slab which looks more exposed than it really is. If there is snow in the Achselrinne then this alternative becomes obligatory. Either way, you will reach a broad, more level scree ledge jokingly nicknamed the Maximilianstrasse (one of Munich's widest main streets). Now it is only 15-20 mins easy scrambling along the loose rock on this ledge and, with the help of wire ropes, over one or two rock slabs to the old summit shelter, the Babenstuber hut, and the new cross beside it. Be warned that the hut is wooden and thus is no protection against lightning.

Under the summit bastion of the Ellmauer Halt.

Descent
a) As ascent.
b) From the Hochgrubachkar combe you can climb up to the Ellmauer Tor gap and down to the Steinerne Rinne (see Route 32).
c) The walk from the Grutten hut to the Gaudeamus hut and from there back to Wochenbrunn is a delightful mountain stroll.
d) The old favourite descent to Hinterbärenbad via the Scharlinger Böden is impassible at present. If you nevertheless find the temptation irresistible, first find out at the Grutten hut precisely what its current condition is.

Difficulty
Comfortable one-day excursion; but only for experienced scramblers who are sure of foot and free from vertigo. Definitely not for novices. Danger from rock-falls on the Gamsänger. Keep your ears open for the rattle of rocks and your eyes open for possible shelter. And cross the dangerous sections as quickly as possible. In early summer parts of the Gamsängersteig path and the grooves beside the Jägerwand and leading up to the Rote-Rinn-Scharte gap may be still under snow, in which case they can be perilously slippery.

Times
Wochenbrunn alm - Grutten hut 1¼-1½ hrs; Grutten hut - Ellmauer Halt 2¼-2½ hrs.

Bases
Grutten hut (1620m; service early June - mid Oct, 50B, 100M, 20L.
Wochenbrunn alm (1087m; restaurant and bar, 22B.

Altitude differences
Ellmau - Wochenbrunn alm 275m; Wochenbrunn alm - Grutten hut 533m; Grutten hut - Ellmauer Halt 724m.

Climbing path altitude
c.550m.

32. HINTERE GOINGER HALT 2192m
Wilder Kaiser

The route I shall be describing approaches both summits from the north, by way of the Stripsenjoch pass and the Steinerne Rinne - the narrow rocky gulch, enclosed on both sides by vertical, indeed often overhanging, walls, which lies at the heart of the Wilder Kaiser and is one of the most memorable locations anywhere in the northern limestone alps.

KAISERGEBIRGE ROUTE 3

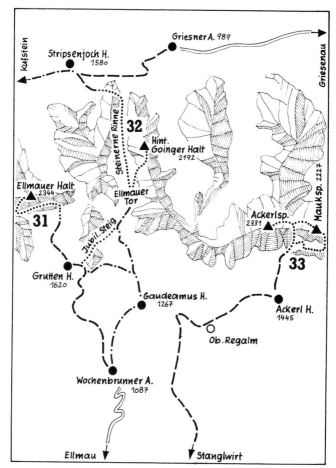

Approach
a) The simplest approach is by the Munich - Innsbruck autobahn to the Kufstein-Nord exit, and then on foot over the Stripsenjoch pass.
b) The walk to the beginning of the climbing path can be reduced by about ¾ hr by making an alternative, and longer, approach by the Munich - Salzburg autobahn to the Bernau exit; from there

*In the Steinerne Rinne, the narrow rocky gulch.
In the background the mighty walls of the Predigstuhls.*

drive via Reit im Winkel and Kössen to the Griesenau and finally, by a toll road, to the Griesner alm (989m).

Ascents to the start of the Eggersteig climbing path
a) Start at Sparchen, on the north-east edge of Kufstein, and walk up the Kaisertal valley. The easy path goes by a series of farms - the Ruppenhof, Zottenhof, Veitenhof and Pfandlhof - to the Anton-Karg-Haus hut (831m) at Hinterbärenbad and on to the Hans-Berger-Haus hut (930m). Now the route begins to climb more steeply to reach the Stripsenjochhaus hut (1580m). From the pass walk east for about 10 mins on the path to the Griesner alm to the sign marking the start of the Eggersteig (at least 4½ hrs from Kufstein).
b) From the Griesner alm (huge car park) it is no more than an easy, comfortable walk to the start of the Eggersteig (c.1¼ hrs).

Summit ascent
The Eggersteig climbing path is positively venerable, dating from 1903/4. It starts across the scree below the Schneeloch crags, traverses diagonally up the slabs of the north ridge of the Fleischbank, and then, about 20 mins from the start, drops some 40m into the actual Steinerne Rinne (1450m). For the next 45 mins our route makes its way up the steep lower part of the gorge, between the massive rock walls to either side, mostly over grass and broken rock, but also zig-zagging on wire ropes and artificial steps up a number of slab pitches. At c.1700m you reach the upper, more level, section of the gorge, which leads, in about 45 mins, to the Ellmauer Tor gap (1995m). From the gap climb east, over scree and boulders, for about 5 mins to join the waymarked path to the summit from the Grutten hut and the Gaudeamus hut to the south. The route continues north, a few metres below the edge of the grassy ridge, first over scree, then on a moderately steep grass slope, until it finally turns up north-eastwards through grassy crags to the summit of the Hintere Goinger Halt.

Descents
a) As ascents.
b) If you do not have to return to a car, you can walk south to the Grutten hut or the Gaudeamus hut (1 hr each). The two paths separate c.25 mins beyond the Ellmauer Tor, where the so-called Jubiläumsweg forks right to the Grutten hut. At each hut there is a signboard to the Wochenbrunner alm, and from there a road takes you down to the village of Ellmau (see Route 31).

KLETTERSTEIG

Difficulty
This is a comfortable day tour from the Griesner alm and a rather more extended one from Kufstein. The Eggersteig and the Steinerne Rinne require surefootedness and freedom from vertigo. Some danger of rock-falls. Only experienced scramblers should venture on the route when some of the wire ropes are still under snow, as is often the case in early summer.

Times
Kufstein - Hinterbärenbad 2½ hrs; Hinterbärenbad - Stripsenjoch 2 hrs; Stripsenjoch - Eggersteig 10 mins; Griesner alm - Eggersteig 1¼ hrs; Eggersteig -Steinerne Rinne - Ellmauer Tor 2 hrs; Ellmauer Tor - Hintere Goinger Halt 30-40 mins.

Bases
Griesner alm (989m); inn; 20B, 10L. Anton-Karg-Haus hut (831m); service early May - mid-Oct, 48B, 62M. Haus hut (930m); summer service; 29B, 45M.
For descent: Grutten hut (1620M); summer service; 10B, 38M, 10L. Gaudeamus hut (1240); service mid-May - mid-Oct; 10B, 49M.

Altitude differences
Kufstein - Stripsenjoch 1100m; Griesner alm - Eggersteig c.460m; Eggersteig - Steinerne Rinne - Ellmauer Tor 545m; Ellmauer Tor - Hintere Goinger Halt 197m.

Climbing path altitude
Steinerne Rinn, lower section 250m.

33. ACKERLSPITZE 2331m AND MAUKSPITZE 2227m
Wilder Kaiser

The summit of the Ackerlspitze curves boldly up above the ridge like a Viking's horn, and it marks both the highest point in the eastern Kaiser and the south-east corner of the ridge enclosing the Griesnerkar combe. The nearby Maukspitze is the summit of the long ridge falling away to the east of the Ackerlspitze and is also the easternmost peak of the whole Wilder Kaiser.

Both summits can be climbed in a single day's very rewarding rock scrambling from the Ackerl hut, by a climbing path which is daringly laid out, but rather sparingly protected with just a few steel rungs.

Approach
The best approach is by the Rosenheim - Kufstein autobahn and then the Wörgl - St.Johann in Tirol road. Turn north by the big restaurant called Stanglwirt onto a side road (signposted 'Prama').

A steep section at the base of the summit tower, made easier by solid iron rings.

KLETTERSTEIG

Ascent to the Ackerl hut

From the Stanglwirt take the Prama road, bear left at the first fork, then continue straight on, past signs to the Grutten hut and the Gaudeamus hut to a barrier at the edge of the woods (1½ km from the Stanglwirt). There is a small parking area at this point with a multitude of prohibition signs, but no signpost. From the barrier walk for about 45 mins up the road, past the pretty, pink Tannbichl chapel to where the road divides into three. Now take the middle track, signposted to the Ackerl hut, cross a stream, continue until you reach a wicket gate, where the track leads into the meadows of the Upper Reg alm (1320m). You can now see the Ackerl hut (1695m), and the remainder of the path is simple and clearly waymarked.

(Note that the hut is unstaffed.)

Summit ascent

The waymarked path starts behind the hut and leads up the grassy tongue through Latschen to a steep combe - which is likely to be snow-filled in early summer. Follow the waymarks where they turn onto a steep, partly grassy spur which projects prominently into the combe. Start up the spur on steel rungs, then traverse round it to your right on ledges which are narrow, exposed, and have no protection. Continue across rubble into the combe, then up to the top couloir. Cross the bergschrund and climb an almost verical rock step with the help of some fixed ring-bolts to get into the couloir. The climb up the couloir is quite easy, thanks to some steel rungs, but beware of rockfalls. When the couloir broadens into a depression - called the Hochsessel - the path, still beautifully waymarked, leads up to the east side, then curves left onto the partly grassy south slope just below the gap. Climb a few yards, and the magnificent view into the Griesner Kar is spread out at your feet. The route turns onto the east side of the summit structure and climbs in hairpins up to the gap at the foot of the summit rocks (2250m). The path leads briefly along the north side of the ridge to the actual rocks. From here the summit is only another 100m higher, involving a delightful, easy little Grade I climb. Just below the summit you will have to squeeze through a cleft onto the north-west side and scramble through some amazing natural rock sculptures to the summit cross a few yards away.

Crossing to the Maukspitze

Return to the bottom of the gap between the two peaks. A little way beyond, branch east and follow the waymarks through a striking natural rock arch to reach the summit in 15-30 mins easy scramble

Descent
Clamber down the simple Flachschneide ridge (Grade I) to the Niedersessel combe, and return to the Ackerl hut as on your ascent.

Difficulty
Straightforward day excursion. Requires surefootedness and freedom from vertigo. Beware of rock-falls.

Times
Going - Ackerl hut 2¾ hrs (or 2-2½ hrs if you drive to the road-barrier); Ackerl hut - Ackerlspitze 2¼ hrs; Ackerlspitze - Maukspitze ¾ hr.

Base
Ackerl hut (1445m); no service; entry only with Alpine Club key; 20M.

Altitude differences
Going - Ackerl hut 915m; Ackerl hut - Ackerlspitze 636m .

Climbing path altitude
c.400m.

34. PYRAMIDENSPITZE 1999m
Zahmer Kaiser

It is the great virtue of the Pyramidenspitze that it combines magnificent views with easy access by almost all of the possible routes. The most spectacular views are across to the cliffs and crags of the north face of the Wilder Kaiser. To the east, where the flat summit falls abruptly away into the Winkelkar, it faces the south of the combe, where the rim is formed by the sheer north walls of the Vordere Kesselschneid, the Hintere Kesselschneid and the Rosskaiser. The protected path described in this Route climbs from the combe through some splendid rockscapes onto the grassy main ridge and the flat, somewhat undefined summit.

Approach
Leave the Inn valley autobahn by the Oberaudorf exit. Drive by way of Niederaudorf to Durchholzen (684m) and turn south by the inn onto a metalled road to the car park by the sign prohibiting motor vehicles.

Ascent
Start gently up the road to the meadows of the Grosspoitneralm (928m), then continue south along a cart track to a fork, where you must bear right for a few more minutes to reach the Winkelalm

KLETTERSTEIG

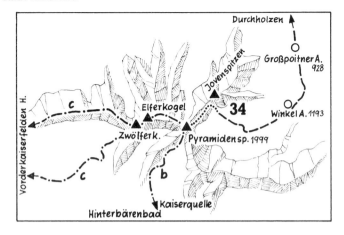

(1193m). The path begins again opposite the alm hut and beyond a small depression. It bears slightly right, up undulating slopes covered by trees and Latschen, into the combe. The combe is divided into two halves - north and south - by a rounded nose of grassy moraine. This ridge is your approach to the foot (at 1600m) of the rock walls of the Jovenspitzen, north-east of the Pyramidenspitze. Now follow the clearly defined path up the crags, first in well protected zig-zags, then over some artificial rock steps, to the gentle grassy slope of the Gamsänger below the ridge connecting the Jovenspitzen to the Pyramidenspitze. The path climbs gently up a green gully to the south-westernmost rocks of the Jovenspitzen, before traversing left to the gap between the two peaks. Continue along the north ridge of the Pyramidenspitze, mostly on the east side, but crossing over to the west side for a short stretch near the top. The final ascent to the summit is by means of some large iron rungs up a steep, smooth slab.

Descents
a) As ascent.
b) South, by way of the Kaiserquelle spring (1463m) and the Kerneck hunting box (1046m) to Hinterbärenbad (892m).
c) Over the summits of the Elferkogel (1916m) and the Zwölferkogel (1846m) to the Vorderkaiserfelden hut (1384m). From there, by way of the Rietzalm, into the Kaisertal valley and to nearby Kufstein.

Do not allow yourself to be tempted by any of the descents to the south, unless you have made some satisfactory arrangement for getting back to your starting point.

Difficulty
Requires a measure of surefootedness and freedom from vertigo. Beware of rock falls from scramblers ahead.

Altitude difference
Durchholzen - Pyramidenspitze c.1300m.

Climbing path altitude
400m

Times
Last car park - summit 3½hrs.

Bases
None. But if descent is made down south side, then Vorderkaiserfelden hut (1384m), German Alpine Club; service all year; 50B, 60M.

Note
In early summer the highest sections of the route are likely to be still under snow.

Protruding, angled steps take one by surprise and wind effortlessly over this rough ground.

Berchtesgaden Alps

35. UNTERSBERG - SALZBURGER HOCHTHRON 1853m
Untersberg

The Untersberg is the northernmost group of the Berchtesgaden alps, and in Germany and Austria it is famous far beyond the circle of mountain-goers because of the wealth of legends and fairy-tales that surrounds it. In addition the mass of caves which it contains, reckoned to number about 200, and of which over 100 have been explored, attract cavers from far and wide.

The Schellenberger Eishöhle - a magnificent ice cave, open to the public - and the 25-year-old cableway from St.Leonhard onto the Geiereck combine to make this familiar Salzburg landmark a popular tourist attraction. The menu here also offers a couple of easily-digested morsels for climbing path enthusiasts, in the shape of the Dopplersteig and the Mittagschartensteig. Both have been so perfectly equipped and protected that they hardly merit the name climbing path; but have the advantage of being safe for any novice with even the slightest freedom from vertigo.

Both paths in succession, with a visit to the cave, make a splendid day tour.

Approach
a) For the Dopplersteig, turn off the Munich - Salzburg autobahn at the Grödig exit, turn right in Grödig and drive 5-10 mins to Glanegg. At the far end of the village, take the narrow road to the Gasthaus Rositten inn, where the Dopplersteig (and another path called the Reitsteig) begin.
b) For the Mittagscharte, drive straight through Grödig to St.Leonhard, then turn onto the main Berchtesgaden road and cross the frontier. 800m beyond the German frontier post, just above the right-hand side of the road, you will see the old watch-

KLETTERSTEIG

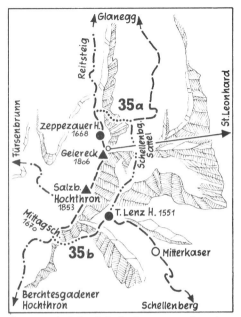

tower that guarded the Schellenberg pass. Stop here at the sign 'Schellenberger Eishöhle', walk about 20 yards up the track and then, at a second signboard to the cave, turn left onto a footpath.

Ascent of the Dopplersteig
Start to the left of the inn, walk to the sign at a rock-fall, and immediately climb steeply to the right. The next section runs above the deep gorge of the turbulent Rossittenbach, which is one of the most picturesque scenes in the Untersberg. The path continues along the side of the valley, through broad-leafed trees and shrubs, climbs some wooden steps and finally crosses the stream to head west towards the rock face. The track which branches right just above the last trees leads to an ice cave called the Kolowratshöhle.

The path continues to the very foot of the almost vertical east wall, where five memorial tablets are set into the rock beside the first artificial steps up the face. The rock section which follows is the climax of the route, and dates all the way back to 1876. The path climbs diagonally up the wall over more than 400 steps cut into the rock to reach the Latschen on the north shoulder of the Geiereck. Parts of this section are rather exposed, but the generous hand-ropes and wire cables up the inside make for a surprisingly easy ascent. Now the path meets the Reitsteig and soon reaches the Zeppezauerhaus hut, from where 20 mins easy walk takes you to the top of the Geiereck (1806m). (Upper station of the cableway, and restaurant next door.) From the Geiereck take the broad footpath south, past the Jungfrauenbrünnl spring, up to the Salzburger Hochthron (1853m; ½ hr), which is the highest summit on the Salzburg side of the Untersberg. Then continue south for 20 mins along clear waymarks, crossing the frontier en route, to the Mittagscharte.

Ascent of the Mittagscharte
From the old watch-tower at the Schellenberg pass, take the waymarked path past the deserted Bachkaser to the shooting-box at the Mitterkaser (1¾ hrs). From here another 1 hr through much prettier landscape takes you to the Schellenberger Eishöhle hut (also called the Toni Lenz hut). Continue on the path to the ice cave until you reach the foot of the south face, just below the cave, where the path divides and you follow the sign for the Mittagscharte. The climbing path up to the gap was constructed in 1934/5. Most of its course up the vertical wall, by way of several tunnels and 450 steps, has been blasted out of the rock. There are windows cut into the tunnels, which present spectacular views both downwards and across to the rocks of the east wall. The whole route has been cut so deep into the rock, and is so carefully protected, that it can be confidently recommended even for relative beginners. The climbing path exits at the Mittagscharte (1670m), at the lowest point of the whole Unterberg range in the gap between the Berchtesgadener Hochthron and the Salzburger Hochthron. A waymarked path leads from the gap to the summit of the Salzburger Hochthron, crossing the frontier on the way (30 mins).

Descents
If you are not combining the Dopplersteig and the Mittagscharte route into a circular excursion, then you can choose between several descent routes.
a) From the Zeppezauerhaus down the Reitsteig to the Gasthaus Rositten. The path goes through woods down hundreds of wooden steps.
b) From the Salzburger Hochthron down the ski-piste, past the Grosser Eiskeller and the Mückenbründl spring, and over the

KLETTERSTEIG

    Schweigmühl alm to Fürstenbrunn (5 mins by car from Glanegg).

c) From the Mittagscharte there is a waymarked ridge path to the Berchtesgadener Hochthron (1973m) - the highest peak in the Untersberg (2 hrs). The Stöhrhaus hut (1894m) makes a convenient base, and is also the starting-point of several descents to Berchtesgaden, Hallthurm (via the Alpensteig path), Greinswies and Ettenberg. There is also a path back to the watch-tower at the Schellenberg pass, where the Mittagscharte ascent begins.

d) From the Schellenberger Eishöhle hut there is a ridge route over the Schellenberger Sattel to the Dopplersteig, which could serve as an alternative connecting link for a round tour. The snag is that this path is at present in rather poor state.

Difficulty
A circular tour of the two climbing paths makes a comfortable day excursion. Or you could go up the Geiereck cableway and scramble down either path in half a day. Both climbing paths require a measure of surefootedness and freedom from vertigo, but are well within the capacities of most beginners.

Times
Gasthaus Rositten - Dopplersteig - Zeppezauerhaus 2½-3½ hrs (or 2½-3 hrs by the Reitsteig); Zeppezauerhaus - Geiereck 20 mins; Geiereck - Salzburger Hochthron 30 mins; Salzburger Hochthron - Mittagscharte 30 mins; Mittagscharte - Berchtesgadener Hochthron 2 hrs; Schellenberg pass watch-tower - Mittagscharte 3½-4½ hrs.

Bases
Zeppezauerhaus hut (1668m); service March-October; 10B, 46M, 15L. Schellenberg Eishöhle hut (Toni Lenz hut) (1551m); summer service; 15B. Stöhrhaus hut (1894m); service Mid May-Mid October; 16B, 45M, 15L; Winter shelter (open) 15M.

Altitude differences
Gasthaus Rositten or Schellenberg pass watch-tower - Salzburger Hochthron c.1370m each.

Climbing path altitudes
Dopplersteig c.150m; Mittagscharte path c.120m.

Notes
Do not miss the opportunity to see the Schellenberger Eishöhle (1570m), the largest ice cave ever discovered in Germany. There are guided tours - from Whitsun to 31 Oct. - every hour, taking ¾-1 hr. In the high season it is best to avoid the rush hours - from about 11.00 to 15.00. None of the other caves can be explored except with special equipment and caving skills. If you possess neither, keep out.

36. HOHER GÖLL   2522m
Göll massif

The climbing path from the Kehlsteinhaus hut to the top of the Gölleiten was equipped in 1957. It opened up for normal mortals the fascinating rockscapes of the Mannlgrat, which had been, until then, the exclusive preserve of rock climbers. It is also the simplest and the loveliest of the normal routes onto the Hoher Göll and, at only 2½ hrs from the Kehlsteinhaus to the summit, the shortest.

Rather unusually, the most exciting sections come, not on the final summit assault, but right at the beginning of the tour.

Approach
The best starting point is the Kehlsteinhaus hut, which is most easily approached from Berchtesgaden. Leave the Munich - Salzburg - Tauern Tunnel autobahn, either at the Bad Reichenhall exit in Germany, or at the Salzburg-Süd exit in Austria, continuing via Grödig.

Ascent to the Kehlsteinhaus
Drive from Berchtesgaden to the Obersalzberg (971m; huge car parks), and take the post bus to the car park on the north side of the Kehlstein (1710m). The first bus leave the Obersalzberg at 8.20; but connoisseurs will take the 'climbers' bus' (actually the Kehlsteinhaus staff bus) which leaves Berchtesgaden station daily at 7.00, or can be picked up at 7.20 at the Obersalzberg.
From the car park at the Kehlsteinhaus to the Kehlstein (1834m) is 10-15 mins walk along a macadam path. For the utterly indolent, there is a huge lift, reached along a tunnel from the car park.

Summit ascent
To reach the start of the climbing path, take the tourist footpath to a signboard pointing the way through a gap in the natural rock wall and onto the ridge, where the first wire ropes await. Squeeze through two tight clefts and then follow the route up and down the rock ridge, changing continually from the east side to the west and back, and neatly circumventing the sheer pinnacles of the Mannlköpfe, until you reach the Mannlscharte gap. A short climb up a dark chimney on steel rungs all too quickly marks the end of the climbing path section. Scramble steeply up to the ridge again, where the route meets the top of the Schusterweg climbing path from the Purtschellerhaus hut.

KLETTERSTEIG

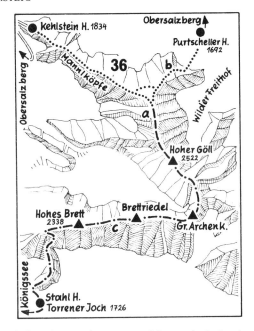

From here it is only 30 mins easy, and increasingly level, walk over loose rock to the summit. There are comprehensive views; indeed on a clear day you should be able to see the Matrashaus hut on the Hochkönig, over 15 miles away.

Descents
a) As ascent. The last post bus leaves the Kehlsteinhaus at 18.20. Should you miss it, the path down to the Obersalzberg begins on the left of the entrance to the lift tunnel.
b) Go back to the junction with the route to the Purtschellerhaus and scramble down the Schusterweg climbing path, which is waymarked and well protected with wire ropes, steel pegs and rungs. Then walk down the east slope, above the Wilder Freithof, to the Eckerfirst (1785m) and on - over what in early summer are dangerously steep snow fields - to the Purtschellerhaus. From there 45 mins walk will take you to the Enzian hut on the Rossfeld road, where you can catch the bus back to the Obersalzberg or go on foot in a further 45 mins.

One of the numerous sharp edges of the ridge of the Hohen Göll. View to the Watzmann and the Hochkalterstock.

KLETTERSTEIG

If you came by car and prefer to be independent of the Kehlsteinhaus bus, park instead at the Ofnerboden - the level stretch of road below the north wall of the Göll. It is 1-1½ hrs walk from here up to the Kehlsteinhaus. But it has the advantage that you can walk back to your car from the Purtschellerhaus in only 1 hr.

c) For a really memorable day, extend your excursion to walk over the top of the whole Göllstock massif. Start down the south-east ridge. Where the ridge divides, take the right-hand branch south-west, then west, over the Kleiner Archenkopf (2381m), the Grosser Archenkopf (2396m) and, after an exposed step which actually is quite simple, the Brettriedel (2342m). From the summit of the Hohes Brett the path (now waymarked) heads down to the Jägerkreuz (2150m) and on to the Torrener Joch pass (1726m). (As a matter of interest, the frontier follows this ridge all the way from the Eckersattel (above the Purtschellerhaus) to the Torrener Joch.) Now leave the ridge and make for the deep-cut Jennersattel gap (1685m) and the Jennergipfel (1874m). Finally an easy walk, or ride down the two-stage cableway, will take you to the railway station at Königssee.

Difficulty
If you go up on the bus and come down by descents a) or b), the ascent of the Göll up the Mannlgrat ridge is a comfortable day tour. Descent c) makes a much longer day. Surefootedness and freedom from vertigo required for the Mannlgrat and the climbing path down to the Purtschellerhaus.

Times
Obersalzberg - Kehlsteinhaus 2 hrs; Kehlsteinhaus - Hoher Göll 2½ hrs; Purtschellerhaus - Hoher Göll 3 hrs; Hoher Göll - Jennergipfel 3-4 hrs; Jennergipfel - Königssee 1-2 hrs.

Bases
Kehlsteinhaus (1834m); no overnight facilities: Purtschellerhaus hut (1692m); service mid May-end October; 15B, 85M.

Altitude differences
Kehlsteinhaus - Hoher Göll 688m; Purtschellerhaus - Hoher Göll 830m; Königssee - Hoher Göll 920m.

Climbing path length
c.1½ km.

37. WATZMANN RIDGE ROUTE (MITTELSPITZE 2713m)

The east wall of the Watzmann is among the classic climbers' routes of the eastern Alps. Similarly the crossing of the Watzmann ridge is one of the finest of high-level excursions for climbing path enthusiasts.

The route has been blasted out in parts, and is so well protected with wire ropes, that experienced scramblers will find it corresponds to no more than climbers' Grade I (easy). But do not attempt the tour without an overnight stop at the Watzmannhaus hut unless you are blessed with quite exceptional stamina.

Approaches
The easiest routes to the Watzmannhaus start on the B305 between Berchtesgaden and Ramsau:
a) From the bus stop at the Wimbachklamm gorge (624m).
b) From the bus stop at Ilsank (578m).
Other alternatives are:
c) Königssee railway station (602m).
d) St Bartholomä on the Königssee (accessible only by water).

Ascents to the Watzmannhaus
The two paths I shall describe meet at the Mitterkaser alm. From there follow the path through bushes and shrubs up the hillside to the Falz alm and then up a long series of hairpins to the Falzköpfl and the Watzmannhaus, which will have been in sight for most of your ascent.
a) The shortest and easiest way up to the Mitterkaser alm goes from the bus stop at the Wimbachklamm. Cross the bridge over the Wimbach and continue, either through the gorge, or, at a signboard, up a wide track through the woods and past the Stubenalm.
b) The path from the bus stop at Ilsank is a little longer. Cross the Ramsauer Ache and walk past the Schapbach-Hof farm to the Gasthaus Hammerstiel (inn) and the Schapbach-Holzstube. Now bear right, climbing a little more steeply through woods, until you meet ascent a) just above the Stubenalm.

Ridge route
From the Watzmannhaus the waymarked path starts, not too steeply at first, up hairpins, then somewhat more steeply up wire ropes over crags to the Schulter (shoulder), and from there runs gently along the ridge to the Hocheck (2657m), where there is a little wooden shelter. This is the most northerly of the three Watzmann peaks, and

KLETTERSTEIG

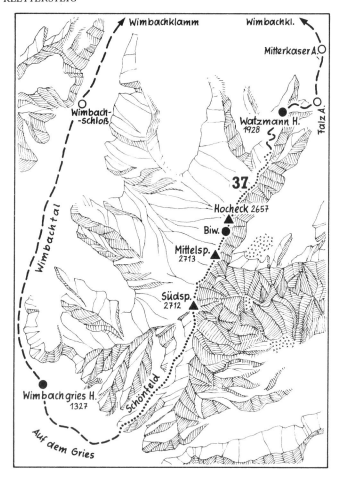

is where the climbing path fun, by now well earned, begins.

From the hut the well-protected route starts down the ridge, some of the way on the sharp edge, at other times just below on the west flank, then climbs again beyond the col. The last section to the Mittelspitze (middle summit) (2713m) goes up a rock terrace on steps cut into the mountain (30 mins from the shelter hut). The next

The Watzmanngrat. View from the Mittelspitze onto the Südspitz, the east wall of the Watzmann to the left.

section, to the Südspitze (south summit) (2712m), is rather more taxing and very exposed, again running along the edge, or just below it on the west side. But it is satisfactorily waymarked and well provided with wire ropes throughout; and it is on this long and rather tricky ridge (Mittelspitze - Südspitze 1½-2 hrs) that experienced scramblers who are footsure and free from vertigo will find their efforts amply rewarded by the adventurous routing of the path and the impressive views.

Descent
From the summit follow the obvious red and yellow waymarks south down the ridge; then, at a gap, bend to the right down the west side, where the route continues down the left side of a steep, wide groove, over some ledges and rock steps, to the top of a vast scree run. Follow the visible tracks down, then bear left over some grassy rock outcrops to the Schönfeld, a small and completely grassy combe. Where the first stream begins, the path heads down through some patches of Latschen and, lower down, past a group of boulders eroded into grotesque shapes, to the valley floor of the upper Wimbachtal. Here it joins the Trischübelsteig and continues more or less level to the Wimbachgrieshütte hut. The walk down the valley from the hut to the bottom of ascent a) is very long, but goes through wonderful scenery, ending with the lovely Wimbachklamm.

Warning. The route is very difficult to navigate in mist. Pay careful attention to waymarks and tracks, especially in the Latschen and low vegetation zone above the trees.

Difficulty
This is definitely not a day excursion. It is fairly strenuous even when it includes an overnight stop at the Watzmannhaus. The ridge route requires absolute surefootedness and freedom from vertigo. All but the most experienced scramblers should consider turning round at the Mittelspitze. Even greater care is required in fresh snow or ice. If thunderstorms threaten, it is advisable to turn round at once!

Times
Wimbachklamm bus stop - Watzmannhaus 3½-4 hrs; Ilsank bus stop - Watzmannhaus 4-4½ hrs; Königssee station - Küroint - Watzmannhaus 3½-4 hrs; St Bartholomä - Küroint - Watzmannhaus 4½-5½ hrs; Watzmannhaus - Hocheck summit 2 hrs; Hocheck - Mittelspitze ½ hr; Mittelspitze - Südspitze 1½-2 hrs; Südspitze - Wimbachgries hut 3 hrs (or not less than 5 hrs for ascent: not recommended!); Wimbachgries hut - Wimbachklamm bus stop 2 hrs.

Bases
Watzmannhaus hut (1928m); service June-30 Sept; 42B, 120M, 35L. Wimbachgries hut (1327m); service all year; 18B, 30M.

Altitude difference
Bridge over the Wimbach - Mittelspitze 2090m; bridge over the Wimbach - Watzmannhaus 1310m; Watzmannhaus - Mittelspitze 780m.

Climbing path length
c.2½ km.

38. SCHÖNFELDSPITZE   2653m
Berchtesgaden alps, Steinernes Meer

The bold, crescent-shaped point of the Schönfeldspitze on the southern edge of the Steinernes Meer is one of the landmarks of the Berchtesgaden alps. The summit offers splendid views over the rock wilderness to the north, and sweeping panoramas towards the Watzmann, the Hochkönig and the distant, snow-covered central Alps. The scramble over the top from the Riemannhaus hut can be accomplished in a day and makes an exciting enterprise.

Approach
From Alm (802m), east of Saalfelden: which is best reached by leaving the Munich - Salzburg autobahn at either the Siegsdorf or the Bad Reichenhall exit and continuing, in either case, via Schneizlreuth.

Ascent to the Riemannhaus
From the pretty village of Alm follow a series of signs 2 km up a metalled road bearing north and towards the mountains. From the beginning of the woods drive another 1.7 km up a dirt road as far as a barrier and park in the large car park. Walk on along the track to the lower station of a goods cableway. Now climb in steep zig-zags up the face of the Sommerstein to the Ramseiderscharte gap. From a distance the face looks impregnable, but the ascent is actually quite easy, up what is really a climbing path in itself, partly cut into the rock and well protected with wire ropes. It requires about the same modest degree of freedom from vertigo as the climbing paths on the Untersberg (Route 35).

Summit ascent
From the Riemannhaus take the waymarked path below the ridge which runs east from the Sommerstein, and head for the gap. The path gradually develops into a climbing path, protected by a small but quite sufficient number of steel rungs. The first section climbs to the gap between the Wurmkopf and the summit. The route then turns to

KLETTERSTEIG

slant up the south side on a rather exposed natural terrace to the crucial moves across a succession of convex slabs, fortunately well protected with steel rungs. The rest is easy; a little climb up a few more steel rungs, up the east slope and then the east ridge, to the summit (2653m), which is marked by a woodcarving of the dead Jesus in the arms of Mary at the foot of the cross, instead of the usual simple cross.

Descents
a) Start down the ascent route, but continue right down the east ridge to the Buchauerscharte gap (2288m). Follow the left-hand track (blue waymarks) down for about 30 mins until you reach the path from Hochbrunnsulzen to the Riemannhaus, which will take you north-west to the southern edge of the Schönfeldgrube combe. At the fork (where the right-hand path leads to the Funtensee) go left and slightly uphill (red waymarks), above the Schönfeldgrube, and round the foot of the Schönfeldspitze back to the Riemannhaus.
b) Start down the ascent route as far as the gap below the Wurmkopf. Now take the ridge running west. If parts of the climbing path look too difficult for a comfortable descent, you can avoid them by escaping onto the north side almost wherever it suits you, but ideally across the larger, lower-lying of the snow-fields. If the weather is fine, continue from the gap along the whole length of the ridge, mostly just to the left of the edge, but in some places following the track a little further down the mountain-side. If you are a collector, you will have no difficulty in picking up the summits of the Streichenbeil (2412m) and the Schöneck (2390m) even though there are no waymarks from the ridge to the tops. And you could add the Sommerstein (2308m) - which stands sentry over the Ramseiderscharte gap - by 20 mins easy scrambling up the waymarked north-west side.

Difficulty
Extended day excursion. Some freedom from vertigo required for both ascent to the hut and summit ascent. Extra care is required on the summit ridge in wet or misty conditions.

Times
To the Riemannhaus from Saalfelden via the Ramseidersteig path, or from Alm, 3½-4 hrs; to the Riemannhaus from the car park by the barrier 2½ hrs; Summit ascent 2½ hrs; Descent 1 hr less by all routes.

Base
Riemannhaus hut (2177m); service Whitsun-early October; 22B, 130M.

The summit block of the Schönfeldspitze from the east.

KLETTERSTEIG

Altitude differences
Alm - Riemannhaus 1375m; Riemannhaus - Schönfeldspitze 476m.

Climbing path altitude
c.200m.

Note
For those unencumbered with a car there are several very popular high-level routes from the Riemannhaus to the following huts: Wiechental hut 2½ hrs; Ingolstädter Haus hut 3 hrs; Wimbachgries hut 6 hrs; St Bartholomä on the Königssee 7 hrs; Kärlingerhaus hut 2½ hrs; Eckbert hut 7 hrs; Bertgen hut 8½ hrs; Matrashaus hut 9½ hrs.

39. HOCHSEILER 2793m
Berchtesgaden alps, Hochkönig massif

The Hochseiler curves up like the back of a whale at the north-west corner of the Hochkönig massif, overlooking the great plateau glacier of the Übergossene Alm, and stretches down to where the ridge is cut by the Torscharte gap. The ridge runs south-east from the summit in several parallel branches. The continuation to the Lammkopf is also called the Hinterthaler Wetterwand, and it is pierced by two gigantic natural rock arches, called the Teufelslöcher (devil's holes) and visible from the south from great distances. The Mooshammersteig -the exciting route that crosses right over the top of the Hochseiler -passes through one of these huge windows.

Approach
From Hinterthal am Hochkönig (1016m): which can be reached by the narrow, winding road from Saalfelden to Bischofshofen, or directly from the Pinzgau valley by an equally narrow road from Lend.

Ascent to the Bertgen hut
a) The ascent I recommend starts on the east side of the stream. Walk for ¾-1 hr along the wide track through woods to a prominent tree with several signboards on it. Branch left on a narrow path up through Latschen and bushes to the Schneekar combe, and continue below the Lammköpfe and across the scree onto the side of the Klammeck. Finally follow the waymarked path up grooves and rock steps to the tiny old, unattended, Bertgen hut (1845m).
b) Alternatively you can reach the Bertgen hut in 3 hrs walk on a

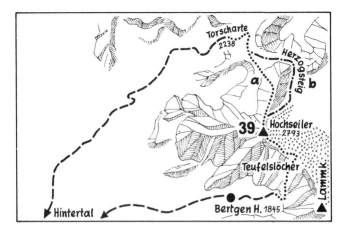

waymarked high-level path from the Erich hut over the Pirch alm.

Summit ascent
From the scree run beside the little snow-field follow the waymarked path up the Schneekar and over the snow. Above the bergschrund follow the wire ropes up the base of the rock wall via a short, wide groove, then slant up to the right over ribs and gullies to a broad ledge (no protection). From here on there is never less than adequate protection. Continue climbing, over slabs, up a boulder-filled depression and then in a series of grooves. In one very shady gully you may find the wire rope buried under old snow. If so, you can by-pass the problem by an easy little climb up the side. Finally scramble up a ridge to reach the climax of this very alpine route, where wire ropes lead through the right-hand arch of the Teufelslöcher to the perpetual snow on the glacier.

If you do not intent to continue up the vast snow-field onto the Hochkönig, then follow the tracks in the snow westwards to the foot of the ridge rocks and, finally, to the eastern corner of the summit mass. The short climb up the grooves and slabs of the east arete is waymarked and well, though economically, protected with steel pegs and rungs. It becomes increasingly exposed, and reaches its most exciting moment where a short, absolutely vertical chimney is climbed on steel pegs. From the top follow the very breezy ridge to the summit.

The Devil's Holes.

Descents

a) Follow the waymarks north-west from the summit down the gently-sloping, rounded ridge. At the lowest point a short path leads down onto the snow-field to join the Herzogsteig path. This is the route for those who feel nervous about attempting the Mooshammersteig descent. But if your courage is high, continue a little way to the top of the Mooshammersteig. The route is prominently waymarked but it is as nature created it, with no artificial protection at all. Still, there is nothing in it that could be rated higher than Grades I and II and, with proper care, experienced climbing path scramblers, provided they are sure of foot and free from vertigo, should experience no difficulties, even without the help of wire ropes. Once at the Torscharte gap (2283m) turn south into the Latschen, where you will find a welcome stream to slake your thirst and ease your feet.

For the best end to this marvellous excursion, avoid the boring dirt road down. Instead take 'Rundweg Nr4' (circular footpath No4) - a delightful path also called the Willi-Schweiger-Weg. Besides being more interesting, it also passes a splendid natural phenomenon - the calcite formations at the Trieffen-Tropfquellen springs.

b) If you decided against the Mooshammersteig and walked down from the gap identified in a) above to the snow-field, you must follow the Herzogsteig. Its route to the Torscharte, along the north-eastern cliffs of the Hochseiler, is well equipped with steps cut into the rock, wire ropes and steel rungs. But even this route requires considerable freedom from vertigo; and in late summer crampons may be required, or ice axes for cutting steps.

Difficulty
This is a long, exhausting tour. It requires fitness, and absolute surefootedness and freedom from vertigo. Only to be attempted in good weather, and not in any circumstances by beginners.

Times
Hinterthal - Bertgen hut 2 hrs; Bertgen hut - Teufelslöcher 2-2½ hrs; Teufelslöcher - Hochseiler 30-45 mins; Hochseiler - Torscharte 1-1½ hrs; Torscharte - Hinterthal 2-3 hrs (or 4½ hrs for ascent).

Base
Bertgen hut (1845m); no service; 22M.

Altitude difference
Hinterthal - Hochseiler 1777m.

Climbing path altitudes
Bertgen hut - Teufelslöcher c.800m; Hochseiler east ridge c.150m; Hochseiler - Torscharte c.450m.

KLETTERSTEIG
40. HOCHKÖNIG 2941m
Berchtesgaden alps

The gleaming white surface of the Übergossene Alm - the only plateau glacier in the eastern alps - is prominently visible from far away to the north. It rises from north to south, and its southern edge is encircled by a crescent of rock crenellations of which the Hochkönig, set more or less in the middle, is the highest. For climbing path scramblers there is a magnificent excursion over the whole mountain, which is the highest in the Berchtesgaden alps. The route climbs either up the Birgkar combe or up the steep south slope and past the Teufelslöcher, then circles round the upper, southern, edge of the glacier, and descends by the popular, much-frequented normal path.

Approach
From the Birgkarhaus hut (1403m), which stands just by the narrow, winding road from Saalfelden to Bischofshofen, just north of the Dientener Sattel. There is also a narrow road to the Dientener Sattel from Lend in the Pinzgau valley.

Ascent to the Erich hut
The Erich hut (1403m), which sits on the south-west slope of the Taghaube near the Schönbergalpe, is the best starting point for the route up the Birgkar. Just walk up the track from the Birgkarhaus (30 mins).

Summit ascents
a) The waymarked path starts through meadows and Latschen, passes the right-hand turning to the Taghaube, and climbs more and more steeply up to the gap to the north of the Taghaube. It is worth stopping here to admire the view down to the Birgkar and up to the summit. Now climb on a long wire rope down a steep, cold and usually snow-filled gully to the Birgkar, where the route meets up with summit ascent b). The path to the foot of the rocks in the combe frequently goes over avalanche remnants. But from there the path is waymarked and clear, as it climbs in steep, tiring hairpins over boulders, slabs, crags and some rock steps, with some wire rope protection in places.

In the upper half of the combe there are often steep snow-fields to cross, which require great care when there is ice or the snow is hard. The top of the topmost snow-field at last brings you to a breach in the circle of rock battlements called the Fensterl

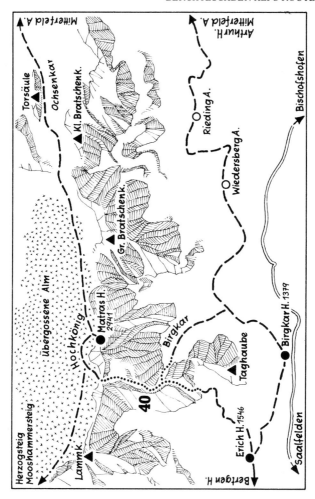

little window). Clamber through, and you are suddenly confronted by the astonishing view over the Übergossene Alm from the eminence of its southern edge. Now walk along a magnificent stretch of snow cornice, then scramble up the harmless summit rocks and along a short length of the ridge to

the Matrashaus hut (2941m).
b) From the Birgkarhaus hut there is an alternative, more direct, route to the bottom of the Birgkar, which goes over the Stegmoos alm and crosses the path from the Arthurhaus hut to the Erich hut. But it is poorly waymarked and more tiring than the route from the Erich hut, so I would not recommend it as a way up.
c) From Hinterthal, however, there is the much more exciting route via the Bertgen hut to the Teufelslöcher, most often used as a route onto the Hochseiler and described in Route 39. From the Teufelslöcher turn east across the glacier (¾-1 hr). This certainly makes a splendid ascent route up the Hochkönig, provided you are not worried about the long trek home. The super-fit could even collect the summit of the Hochseiler before turning their attention to the Hochkönig (again see Route 39).

Descents
a) The obvious choice is the easy, popular, scenically very rewarding normal path. Start by following waymarks and a wire rope down a short cleft to a little buttress projecting from the summit rocks. From here take an almost level line across the glacier, past the sign for the Schweitzerweg, to the gap where the path goes over the edge and starts its descent. Make your way down through scree to the north-east corner of the foot of the Kleiner Bratschenkopf, where there is a hidden, crystal-clear spring, and on, over boulders, to the foot of the formidable Torsäule.
   Continue down into the Ochsenkar combe, then through shrubs and bushes below one of the vertical faces of the Manndlwand to reach the Mitterfeld alm (1668m). From here a comfortable path leads to the Arthurhaus hut (1503m). If you are exceptionally endowed with stamina, you may feel like finishing along the high path to the Birgkarhaus or the Erich hut via the Rieding alm and the Wiedersberg alm. Most people, however, will prefer to return by road via Mühlbach; but note that public transport connections are very poor.
b) As ascent
c) From the summit take the route west, then continue via the Mooshammersteig climbing path to the Bertgen hut and return to the Erich hut by the high path over the Posch alm and the Pichl alm (see Route 39).
d) To Hinterthal by the Herzogsteig climbing path and the Torscharte (see Route 39).

The protected passage allowing entrance into the Birgkar.

KLETTERSTEIG

Difficulty
Strenuous day tour. The ascent up the Birgkar requires freedom from vertigo and, more importantly, surefootedness and experience on steep and possibly icy snow-fields. Descents c) and d) both require exceptional stamina.

Times
Birgkarhaus hut - Erich hut ½ hr; Erich hut - Matrashaus hut 4-5 hrs; Birgkarhaus hut - Matrashaus hut via Stegmoos alm 5½ hrs; Matrashaus hut -Arthurhaus hut 3-3½ hrs (or 5 hrs for ascent); Arthurhaus hut - Birgkarhaus hut by the high path 2 hrs.

Bases
Erich hut (1546m); service mid June-mid Oct; 6B, 14M, 6L. Matrashaus on the Hochkönig (2941m) burnt down in May 1982. Emergency bivouac facilities only. Mitterfeld alm (1668m); service all year; 14B, 27M. Arthurhaus hut (1502m); service all year; 6B, 54M. On the way down from the Arthurhaus to Mühlbach: Hochkeilhaus hut (sister hut to the Arthurhaus) (1400m); 50B, 15M. Mandlwandhaus hut (1330m) service all year; 20B, 40L. Rupertihaus hut (1265m); service all year; 40B. Kopp hut (1307m); service all year; 8B, 10M.

Altitude differences
Birgkarhaus - Matrashaus 1538m; Arthurhaus - Matrashaus 1439m.

Climbing path altitude
c.700m.

41: PERSAILHORN 2347m
Berchtesgaden Alps

The four-square mass of the Persailhorn stands outside the western rim of the Steinernes Meer. Consequently the summit commands some interesting views: west across the Salzach valley to the Leoganger Steinberge, and south-west to the distant Hohe Tauern and the Venediger massif.

The summit has only recently been made accessible to scramblers by the installation of a climbing path. If, moreover, you are long on experience and short on timidity, you can continue beyond the summit to a further spectacular - but, it must be said, extraordinarily exposed - adventure. The Saalfeldener Höhenweg is a clearly waymarked but unprotected route over the various summits along the ridge connecting the Persailhorn with the Breithorn.

Approach
From Bad Reichenhall or Kufstein, drive to Saalfelden. Then follow the Bundestrasse towards Lofer, but turn off to the right at Pabing and follow signposts to Bachwinkl (840m). Continue through the village to the Ofenbach (stream) and the car park.

Ascent to the Peter Wiechenthaler hut

At the car park, look for the signpost for the Öfenbachsteig path, which winds in hairpins up the Kienberg to a crossing of paths in the depression between the Kienberg and the Kienalpkopf (1320m). Stroll straight on to the hut (1752m), which overlooks the southern edge of the Steinernes Meer.

Summit ascent

The waymarked path from the hut leads east through latschen, then rises steeply to the entrance to the climbing path at the foot of the west face of the summit massif of the Persailhorn. The route follows a distinct track south, skirting the bottom of the rock wall, to reach the foot of the south ridge. Climb the ladders up the first section of the ridge, then traverse west along rock ledges to a very exposed stance. Now turn south and climb again: up a gully almost as tight as a chimney; then onto the shoulder of the summit ridge; finally over large slabs to the summit. Except only for a few very short interruptions, the whole climbing path, from entrance to exit, is well protected. Some of the most exposed places are eased by iron rungs or lengths of iron ladder. Moreover, the route has been so cleverly laid across the mountain that there is virtually no danger of rock-falls caused by scramblers already higher up.

Descents

a) As ascent.
b) As ascent as far as c.250m before the Peter Wiechenthaler hut, where a comfortable waymarked path branches left. Follow it (and its occasional wire ropes) down the western side of the Persailhorn, through Latschen and across some huge scree-runs, down to the Steinalm (1271m; service until mid October). Just beyond the alm hut a path goes over the shoulder and down the wooded Lärchenriedl back to the Öfenbach valley and the car park.
c) Via the Saalfeldener Höhenweg, for a genuinely alpine excursion. The route takes in two additional summits and is without any protection from end to end. Be under no illusions. This is an outing only for the most experienced scramblers, blessed with total freedom from vertigo and perfect surefootedness, and who also have some climbing skills.

From the summit of the Persailhorn, continue east along the ridge. Follow the waymarks down the north flank, then over slabs and across gullies back onto the ridge, to a memorial cross

Klettersteig on the Persailhorn.

(called the Kropsch cross). Scramble very carefully up some scree covered ledges to the summit of the Mitterhorn (2491m; 1½-2hrs). Take a well earned rest at this point and savour the magnificent view across the south-western sector of the Steinernes Meer, bounded to the north by the Grosser Hundstod (2594m) and to the south-west by the striking form of the Schönfeldspitze (2653m). The waymarks lead on towards the Breithorn. Follow them down the ridge, then onto the south side down a section of rock slabs with very few hand-holds. Traverse round the foot of the Drei Docke to the slabs of a wide, descending ridge. Continue your traverse along a ledge round the south side of the Kleine Docke, and finally climb straight up again to reach the summit (1½hrs).

Your descent is to the Riemannhaus hut, by way of the path down to the lower station of the goods cableway. From there, bear right along the Ramseider Steig path, past Schloss Lichtenberg, and so back to the car park at Bachwinkl.

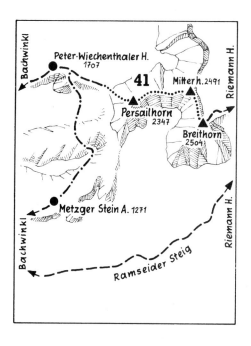

KLETTERSTEIG

Difficulty
a) The climbing path is a comfortable day excursion. It presents no great difficulties, and may be attempted even when the weather is a little uncertain.
b) Add the Saalfeldener Höhenweg (Grade II) and you are in for a very long and exhausting day tour. To shorten it a little you could end it with an overnight stop at the Riemannhaus hut, and use the next day to climb the Schönfeldspitze. Freedom from vertigo and surefootedness are essential for this route. Extra care is required in wet conditions. If there is mist, do not even attempt the route.

Altitude differences
Bachwinkl - Peter Wiechenthaler hut 912m; Peter Wiechenthaler hut - Persailhorn 595m; Persailhorn - Mitterhorn - Breithorn 157m.

Climbing path altitude
c.450m

Times
a) and b): Bachwinkl - Peter Wiechenthaler hut 2-2½hrs; Peter Wiechenthaler hut - Persailhorn 2½-3hrs. c): Persailhorn - Mitterhorn 1½-2hrs; Mitterhorn - Breithorn 1½-2hrs; Breithorn - Riemannhaus hut 1hr; Riemannhaus - Ramseider Steig path - Bachwinkl 3 hrs.

Bases
Peter Wiechenthaler hut (1752m), Austrian Alpine Club: service June - end September; 25B, 40M: Riemannhaus hut (2177m), German Alpine Club; service Easter, then Whitsun - early October; 22B, 60M, 16L.

Dachstein

42. HOHER DACHSTEIN 2996m

The Hoher Dachstein is the highest summit of any of the tours described in this book, and the second highest mountain in the northern limestone alps. In fine weather, the passage over the whole mountain - over glaciers, up the north-east side, then down the west ridge and, after more glacier work, through the Steinerscharte gap - is one of the finest ice and rock excursions any climbing path enthusiast can hope to experience. To reach the summit used to require long treks to and from one or other of the base huts, but since the opening of the cableway from the Ramsau valley to the top of the Schladming glacier, the whole tour can be comfortably fitted into one day.

Approach
a) Via the Ramsau glacier cableway. Leave the Salzburg - Tauern Tunnel autobahn at the Radstadt exit, take the main road to Radstadt and Schladming, then turn left onto a minor road to Ramsau and finally take a toll road to the lower station at the Türlwand hut (1710m).
b) Via Obertraun. Leave the autobahn at the Golling exit. Take the main road to Abtenau, over the Pass Gschütt, to the Hallstätter See, then turn right to Hallstatt and Obertraun (608m).
c) As b), but turn right at Gosau and drive 7 km to the last car park at the Vorderer Gosausee (933m).

Ascent to the Hunerkogel
a) The quickest and most comfortable way to scale the 1000m or so to the Hunerkogel is by the Gletscherbahn Ramsau cableway (also known as the Dachstein-Südwandbahn). If you plan to take the first trip at 8.00 during the high season, you will need to be in the queue at least ½ hr earlier.
b) From Obertraun take all three sections of the Dachsteinbahn cableway - up to the intermediate stations at the Dachsteinhöhlen caves (1350m) and the Krippenstein (2079m) and down again to the Gjaid alm (1791m). From the third station, or from the Schilcherhaus hut 15 mins down the hill, the route begins

southwards in a series of steep ups and downs over the Niederer-, Hoher- and Kleiner Gjaidstein (2483m, 2792m and 2735m), then leads down into the Gjaidsteinsattel gap (2647m). From there cross the Schladming glacier to the Hunerkogel.

c) From the Vorderer Gosausee take the delightful, level track to the Gosau-Lacke tarn and then continue up a footpath to the Hinterer Gosausee (1154m; 1½ hrs). From here reckon 3½ hrs on a tiring and sometimes very steep waymarked path to the Adamek hut (2196m) just below the north-west edge of the glacier, the Grosser Gosau-Gletscher. From the hut the walk to the Steinerscharte gap will take another 2 hrs. This section goes mostly across the glacier, so it is advisable to check on conditions with the hut warden. In mist, great care is required. From the Steinerscharte the best route over the Dachstein is up the west ridge (see summit ascent a).

Summit ascents

a) Ascent of the north-east slopes, along the bergschrund: From the Hunerkogel the route starts with a magnificent 40 mins of glacier crossing, first gently down the Schladming glacier, then across the adjoining Hallstatt glacier and up the snow combe at the foot of the Dirndln. Climb steadily along the edge of the combe and up to the Dachsteinwarte hut, called after a small eminence below the east ridge of the Hoher Dachstein and at the edge of the sheer south face of the Dachstein plateau.

From the hut follow the tracks north-west across the snow and up the glacier, keeping close to the rock edge, until you reach the bottom of the rock couloir running down from the summit. Depending on conditions, make the crossing of the bergschrund either directly below the couloir or a little to the right. Once over the bergschrund, climb up a short, steep hard snow slope or, if you made the crossing on the right, climb up rock steps, to the Mecklenburgstein (memorial tablet), where the actual couloir begins and where summit ascent b) joins from the left along a ledge.

Now climb steeply and with help from wire ropes and steel rungs, partly up good rock in the couloir but mainly up the right-hand edge. At one spot - 20-30m below the summit - where the protection is rather exiguous, the climbing is Grade II.

b) Ascent up the rock:
This is an alternative route, over a horizontal section of the east ridge called the Schulter (shoulder), which avoids the climb up

The west ridge of the Hoher Dachsteins from the highest Gosaugletscher.

the glacier to the foot of the summit couloir. It is definitely preferable to summit ascent a) when heavy thaws have widened the bergschrund.

From the Dachsteinwarte hut head north-west to the foot of a rock spur which points down from the Schulter and projects north-east. The bergschrund is normally easy to cross at this point. Now climb the wire ropes which lead up to the spur and diagonally to the right onto the level Schulter. Cross some slabs and a snow-field to the foot of the north wall that rises to the east ridge, negotiate a rock step onto a sizeable platform and then climb straight up over some more rock steps to a memorial tablet. Finally turn right, down a sloping ledge with an overhang of black rock, then across a steep and often icy snow-field, to meet summit ascent a) at the Mecklenburgstein.

Descents

a) The west ridge offers both magnificent scenery and the most moderate gradients, which makes it an ideal descent. From the summit cross, the route starts along the exposed top section of the west ridge to a gap and then leads easily down from the ridge, over rock steps and slabs, to the top of the first wire ropes. Follow them in hairpins down the north slope, over one steep rock step, and down to the foot of the west ridge, which falls away from the Obere Windlucke (2746m) - the gap between the Hoher Dachstein and the Mitterspitze.

Now follow the tracks in the snow down the east side of the Grosser Gosau-Gletscher to meet the path from the Adamek hut (waymarked No.601) and turn to cross the bergschrund below the Steinerscharte gap. The first, vertical section of the rock face is easily climbed thanks to a long steel ladder. Scramble diagonally left to a scree gully and then on wire ropes up the gully and over some rock steps and slabs to the Steinerscharte (15 mins from bergschrund).

From the gap make the easy descent eastwards down the wire ropes to the Hallstatt glacier. Follow the tracks eastwards and more or less level, past the Niederer Dachstein, then swing south and climb steadily back to the Dachsteinwarte hut and the Hunerkogel (1 hr from Steinerscharte).

b) From the Obere Windlucke to the foot of the Steinerscharte as for descent a), but then left over the Grosser Gosau-Gletscher to the Adamek hut (see ascent c).

c) If your stamina is not exhausted and your surefootedness and freedom from vertigo are in good shape, you could spurn the temptation of the cable-car ride down and, instead, scramble down via the Hunerscharte gap (2-2½ hrs).

Difficulty
A true high alpine expedition. If you travel up on the cableway, it fits comfortably into one day. From the Gosau lakes, and even from the Gjaid alm, it would be beyond most people's powers to complete the tour in a day, and an overnight stop is essential. All the summit ascent routes and the descent from the Hunerkogel require surefootedness and freedom from vertigo. The summit couloir additionally requires some basic climbing skills. Novices, children and the nervous should be roped. Not to be undertaken in mist!

Times
Hunerkogel - Dachsteinwarte hut 40 mins; Dachsteinwarte hut - Hoher Dachstein, by either ascent route, 1 hr; descent down the west ridge ½-¾ hr (or 1 hr for ascent); Obere Windlucke - Steinerscharte - Dachsteinwarte hut 1½ hrs; Gjaid alm - Hunerkogel 5½ hrs; Vorderer Gosausee - Adamek hut 5 hrs; Adamek hut - Steinerscharte - Dachsteinwarte hut 3 hrs.

Bases
Upper station of the Ramsauer Gletscherbahn cableway on the Hunerkogel (2685m); restaurant and bar service all year; no overnight facilities. Dachsteinwarte hut (2740m); service mid-April-mid-Sept; 25B, 48M. Adamek hut (2196m); service over Easter, then Whitsun-end Sept; 27B, 48M, 6L. Schilcherhaus hut (1739m); service all year; 32B, 60M.

Altitude difference
Lower cableway station - Hunerkogel 975m; Hunerkogel - Hoher Dachstein 311m; Gjaid alm - Hoher Dachstein 1264m (plus many substantial counter-climbs!); Vorderer Gosausee - Hoher Dachstein 2003m.

Climbing path altitudes
West ridge, north-east slope (bergschrund) ascent, and ascent up the rocks, each 250m; Steinerscharte from either side c.50m.

Note
If your approach is via Obertraun, visit the famous ice cave, the Dachstein-Rieseneishöhle, and the nearby Mammuthöhle (mammoths' cave). If you have a little more time to spare, add a visit to the Koppenbrüllerhöhle, with its spectacular stalagmites and stalactites (3 km east of Obertraun, by the Gasthaus Koppenrast inn). The guided tours of all the caves operate mid-May-mid-Oct.

43. KOPPENKARSTEIN 2865m

Like many secondary summits, the long rock ridge east of the Hunerscharte is overshadowed in fame and public esteem by its big brother, the Hoher Dachstein. Most people who ride up to the Hunerscharte do so to make the pilgrimage to 'the summit' to the west. But if you can make time for the Koppenkarstein, you will enjoy a very satisfying additional rock tour and different, but equally fine, views. And on occasions when doubtful weather forbids access to the main summit - especially when conditions on the northern rock approaches are icy - the Koppenkarstein is the ideal alternative.

Approaches
See Route 42.

Ascent to the Hunerkogel
See Route 42.

Summit ascent
From the Hunerscharte gap start east up the waymarked ridge to a painted arrow 100-200m short of the air traffic beacon. Branch left, and you will soon join waymarks leading down to the northern foot of the rock. (Do not follow the climbing path which you see continuing along the ridge. It leads only as far as the air traffic beacon, beyond which progress along the ridge becomes impossible.) Follow the foot of the wall a little way, then climb on wire ropes and some steel rungs up the north slope. This section starts very steeply, then flattens out somewhat; and it by-passes the impassible part of the ridge above. The route reaches the ridge again at the Austriascharte gap (2704m), where it meets descent b) coming up from the south, then follows the ridge a short distance to a second gap, the Hinteres Türl (2622m). (Mjr Absalon-Weig has kindly drawn my attention to the fact that this gap provides a convenient crossing from the Edelgriess to the Schladming glacier.)

From the gap progress is surprisingly easy up some artificially-widened ledges on the south side of the mountain to the cairn on the lower summit. Now climb down two steep ladders on the south-east flank, then up to the ridge again, briefly along the ridge, and down again on the north side, where a slanting natural window opens a surprise view through the ridge. Cross the ridge once more, then climb steeply up the south side to a little hump supporting a goods cableway pylon. The final length of ridge is well protected, and soon reaches the research buildings on the summit, and the tiny, unattended Miki hut - an emergency shelter which, in its time, has no doubt provided relief for all sorts of emergencies.

Descents
a)   Return to the Austriascharte, then follow the waymarks down the

*The face climb on the Koppenkarstein.
Although of massive proportions the route is kindly,
yet snow and verglas demand prudence.*

south side and cross the hard snow on the Edelgriessgletscher glacier to reach the ridge to the Edelgriesshöhe. At the fork where the path to the Guttenberghaus hut branches left, keep right. This is the path south, towards the Austria hut. Follow it down the steep slope, zig-zagging some of the way, and through the Edelgriess combe. Some distance before you reach the hut, branch right to the lower station of the cableway.

b) Return to the Hunerscharte, then scramble down the climbing path to the lower station of the cableway.
c) Return to the Hunerscharte, then walk up to the upper station of the cableway and ride down.

Difficulty
High alpine excursion. If you ride both ways on the cable-car, can be fitted into a half day; if you ride up but walk down, makes a comfortable day-tour. Requires surefootedness and freedom from vertigo.

Times
Hunerkogel - Koppenkarstein c.1-1½ hrs; descent from Hunerkogel to cableway lower station 2-2½ hrs; for other times see Route 42.

Bases
Miki hut on summit (2865m); unattended; open emergency shelter: for other possibilities see Route 42.

Altitude differences
Hunerscharte - Koppenkarstein 252m; for other figures see Route 42.

Climbing path altitude
From Hunerkogel c.250m.

Salzkammergut
44. TRAUNSTEIN 1691m

The most northerly projection of the northern limestone alps into the pre-alpine plain is the arresting rock form of the Traunstein. The Naturfreundesteig (nature lovers' path), equipped nearly 60 years ago, traces a cunning route from virtually by the shore of the Traunsee up the steep west face of the Traunstein. It is an enchanting path, and a perfect showcase for the scenic variety of the Salzkammergut. The view embraces the expansive plain to the north, the shimmering glaciers on the Dachstein, the dolomitic pinnacles of the Gosau ridge to the south, the deep blue of the lake 1200m below, and the bright white sails which speckle its surface. What could make a more perfect autumn ending to a summer on the climbing paths?

Approach
Leave the Salzburg - Vienna autobahn at the Regau exit, then drive to Gmunden and another 5 km along the east shore of the Traunsee to the barrier near the Jausenstation Moaristidl (cafe) (425m; several small parking places).

Summit ascents
a) Naturfreundesteig:

From the first barrier walk for 15 mins up the track to a second, then, a few yards beyond, bear left into the trees on a waymarked path to the foot of the vertical west wall. Walk a little way along the foot of the wall (beware of rock-falls) to the official start of the Naturfreundesteig at a memorial tablet. Climb two long ladders over the most difficult sections of a very steep, grassy rock spur. The excellent protection continues; in fact some of the wire ropes at this low altitude are anchored to thick pine trunks as the path makes its way south-east, up steep hairpins, through the mighty trees. Continue up the steep grassy face on exposed ledges, past the so-called Band (terrace) and Pechgraben (misfortune gully), and from the foot of a rock overhang climb the section called the Lenziger Leiter (Lenzing ladder). The next section is called the Überstieg (crossing) and takes you over onto the south side. Now the route is easier, as it turns north-east to the Schöne Rast (lovely rest), then continues over awkward scree through the Latschen. After a short level section to a rock projection called the Böses Eck (nasty corner), climb right, on wire ropes up a steep groove and through a natural rock arch, which is the last thrill of the tour. As you climb through, look back for a final dizzy view down, then turn towards the red-white-and-red Austrian flag fluttering from the Traunstein hut (1581m), which you will reach in 15-20 mins easy scramble on wire ropes. The summit is another 110m higher, and the 30 mins easy walk takes you past the top of the Hernlersteig and the Gmunden hut (1666m).

b) This is the less interesting of the two paths. The start is clearly signposted at the side of the road, c.750m before the first barrier. The path heads into the woods, passes the signposted fork to the Dürrenberg and the Laudachsee, goes through the Kaltenbachwildnis (Kaltenbach wilderness), and after 15-20 mins reaches the foot of the rock face. Now climb to your right (to the south-east) up two slanting ladders and then on wire ropes up to a more comfortable forest path, which will take you to a platform with a fine view towards the Dachstein (c.1 hr from the start). Continue east, out of the forest and into the Latschen, to a wide rock gully. Climb up the wire ropes to the level ridge and enjoy your first view over the expanse of the plain to the north and to the flag by the Gmunden hut just to the south. A few minutes walk will take you to the gap by the hut, and a further 15 mins, through Latschen, to the summit.

Descents

As ascents. The Hernlersteig is shaded, and therefore cooler, in the morning, and may therefore be the better ascent, especially in high summer. The magnificent views from the more interesting Naturfreundesteig are perhaps easier to savour on the way down.

Difficulty

Average day excursion. Some surefootedness and freedom from vertigo required for the Hernlersteig and rather more for the Naturfreundesteig.

Times

Traunsee shore - Traunstein, by either route 3-3½ hrs.

Bases

Traunstein hut (1581m); service May-Sept; 26M. Gmunden hut (1666m); service 1 May-31 Oct; 2B, 47L.

Altitude difference

Traunsee shore - Traunstein 1266m.

Climbing through the window of the Naturfreundesteiges.

KLETTERSTEIG

Climbing path altitudes
Hernlersteig c.300m wire ropes; Naturfreundesteig c.600m wire ropes.
Note
Take time to look at Gmunden, and especially to visit the country palace and the lakeside palace at Ort.

IF YOU LIKE ADVENTUROUS ACTIVITIES ON MOUNTAINS OR HILLS YOU WILL ENJOY READING:

CLIMBER

MOUNTAINEERING/HILLWALKING/TREKKING SCRAMBLING/ROCK CLIMBING/ IN BRITAIN AND ABROAD

AVAILABLE FROM NEWSAGENTS, OUTDOOR EQUIPMENT SHOPS, OR BY SUBSRIPTION (6-12 MONTHS) FROM HOLMES MCDOUGALL LTD., RAVENSEFT HOUSE, 302-304 ST. VINCENT'S STREET, GLASGOW G2 5RG

THE WALKERS' MAGAZINE

the great OUTDOORS

COMPULSIVE MONTHLY READING FOR ANYONE INTERESTED IN WALKING

Available from your newsagent, outdoor equipment shop or on subscription from:
Holmes McDougall Ltd., Ravenseft House, 302/304 St. Vincent Street, Glasgow G2/5NL

Printed by Carnmor Print & Design,
95/97, London Road, Preston, Lancashire.

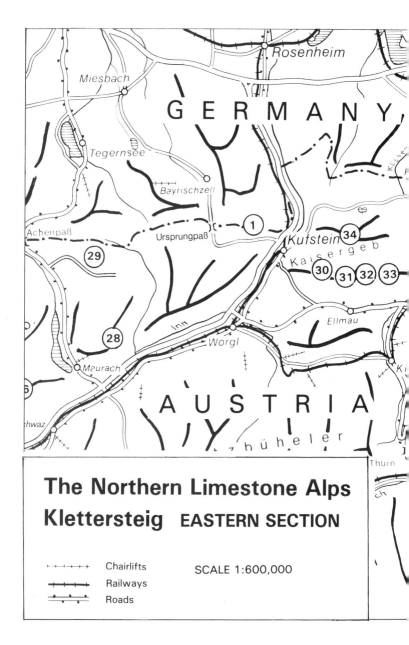